*quick & easy*
# 20-minute meals
## IN COLOUR

## catherine atkinson

# foulsham

The Publishing House, Bennetts Close, Cippenham, Slough,
Berkshire, SL1 5AP, England

Foulsham books can be found in all good bookshops and direct from
www.foulsham.com

ISBN: 978-0-572-03486-3

Copyright © 2008 The National Magazine Company Limited

Photographs © The National Magazine Company Limited

A CIP record for this book is available from the British Library

Printed in Dubai

# Contents

# Introduction

After a busy day out or at work, the last thing anyone wants to do is spend hours in the kitchen. Although most of us enjoy good food and aspire to eating a healthy diet, our hectic lives and limited time can make it difficult to be inspired to create tasty dishes made from fresh ingredients, properly cooked and not simply reheated in the microwave. But there's really no need to resort to tasteless supermarket ready-meals and high-fat takeaways.

This cookbook provides the perfect solution – no-fuss food that's easy to make, looks good and tastes delicious. Here you'll find main meal recipes that can all be prepared and cooked in around 20 minutes or even less – invaluable if you are stretched for time. In addition, there are lots of helpful tips with many of the recipes, plus variations and ways to make cooking even quicker and easier.

There are mouth-watering meals to suit every occasion, from mid-week meals to more special weekend dining. You'll also find a selection of snacks and light meals that are perfect for lunches or super-quick suppers, and lots of suggestions for delectable desserts and advice on healthy eating and stocking up your storecupboard. With a little forward planning, you can create delicious simple meals from fresh ingredients every day of the week.

# Why bother to cook?

The underlying message of all good nutritional advice is that it doesn't matter what you eat occasionally; what matters is what you eat most of the time. It is fine to tuck into a takeaway or a decadent dessert now and then, but it's important to balance this by mainly eating meals made from a variety of freshly prepared foods.

Although medical and nutritional knowledge has advanced in the last few decades and most of us are aware of what the experts advise, putting that advice into practice hasn't necessarily followed; obesity is on the increase and most of us eat far more sugar, salt and saturated fat than we should. What you eat can influence your health in many ways; as well as providing resistance to infection and serious diseases, eating a balanced diet will make you feel great, look good and give you lots of energy.

A balanced diet is one that supplies the body with protein, energy, fibre and vitamins and minerals in sufficient but not excessive amounts. Achieving this often means juggling what we know we should eat with foods we enjoy and that suit our lifestyle. Current guidelines are that most of us should eat more starchy foods, more fruit and vegetables, a little less meat and a lot fewer fatty and sugary foods. Supermarket ready-meals often make nutritional claims, such as 'lower-fat' or 'reduced-calorie', but few provide the balance of nutrients or the flavour of a freshly prepared meal. Try to make meal preparation and eating together part of your family routine – it's good both nutritionally and socially – even if you can't manage it every day.

# Five easy steps to healthy eating

### PROTEIN

Protein is needed for both growth and repair. Get most of your protein from poultry, fish and seafood, vegetarian food and small amounts of red meat, which also provides iron to prevent anaemia and zinc for growth and healthy skin and bones, but which is high in saturated fat so shouldn't be eaten every day.

### DAIRY

Dairy products (or dairy-free alternatives such as soya milk and soya yoghurt) and eggs are valuable in a healthy diet. Dairy foods are a vital source of calcium, important for strong bones and teeth and a healthy nervous system. This mineral is particularly important for women throughout life to prevent the development of osteoporosis. To reduce fat intake, try to choose lower-fat versions such as skimmed or semi-skimmed milk.

### COMPLEX CARBOHYDRATES

Eat more starchy carbohydrates. Around half of the calories in a healthy diet should come from complex carbohydrates and most of this from starchy foods – bread, potatoes and other starchy vegetables, pasta, rice and cereals. These are only 'fattening' if smothered in butter or fried. Starchy carbohydrates provide lots of energy, some protein and essential vitamins and minerals, especially from the B group, which are crucial for healthy nerves and digestion. Try to eat as wide a variety as possible, choosing wholegrain and wholemeal types as often as you can.

### FRUIT AND VEGETABLES

A third of your food should consist of fresh fruit and vegetables. Eat five portions a day as they provide lots of vitamin C for healing and immunity and other antioxidant vitamins and minerals. These help prevent harmful free radicals in the body initiating or accelerating diseases such as cancer, heart disease and arthritis and can also slightly reduce sun damage and ageing.

### PROCESSED FOODS

Avoid too many processed foods. Cut down on meat products and eat items such as sausages, hot dogs, burgers, pâtés, salami and meat pies no more than once a week as they contain large amounts of saturated fats and often undesirable additives.

# Your quick & easy storecupboard

There are few things worse than returning home after a tiring day to an empty food cupboard and fridge and wondering what on earth you are going to eat. However, if you invest in a few basics, you'll always have some standbys to rustle up a delicious dinner in minutes. It will also mean less shopping and you will have the ingredients to inspire your creativity when you want to improvise.

Try to keep your ingredients tidy; arrange items logically, so you can see at a glance if you have what you need, and throw away items that are out of date. Obviously, the size of your kitchen cupboards, fridge and freezer will determine the amount and number of items you can store. There's no need to buy everything on the list; instead build up your store gradually, choosing the ingredients you use a lot of and those for recipes you'd like to cook.

## ▨ STAPLES

- **Couscous:** Good for serving with spicy dishes and only needs brief soaking in boiling water or stock.
- **Dried pasta:** Spaghetti and a couple of your favourite pasta shapes. For speed, choose 'quick-cook' versions that take only 4–5 minutes to cook.
- **Egg noodles:** Fine egg noodles take only 3 minutes to cook, medium 4 minutes. 'Straight-to-wok' noodles are brilliant for adding to stir-fries at the last minute and only need to be warmed through.
- **Pizza bases:** Long-life or frozen.
- **Plain (all-purpose) and self-raising flour and cornflour (cornstarch):** For baking, coating ingredients and thickening sauces.
- **Rice:** 'Easy-cook' long-grain and basmati rice produce perfect results every time. You can also buy boil-in-the-bag rice and microwavable brown basmati that will be ready in 2 minutes (rather than the usual 20 minutes when cooking from scratch).

## ▨ CANS, JARS AND BOTTLES

- **Beans:** Including baked beans and pulses such as red kidney beans and borlotti beans. Can be used to make meat dishes go further or for high-protein vegetarian meals.
- **Chopped plum tomatoes:** Plain or with added ingredients such as chillies, garlic or herbs. Excellent for simple pasta sauces (see page 12).
- **Green and red pesto:** Especially good in pasta dishes.
- **Hoisin sauce:** A marinade and baste, and a dip for Chinese snacks.
- **Mayonnaise:** For dips and dressings.

- **Roasted red (bell) peppers and stoned (pitted) olives in oil:** Great for pizza toppings and bruschetta.
- **Sweet chilli sauce:** A sweet fruity sauce used as a flavouring and a dip.
- **Sweetcorn and potatoes:** Invaluable when you haven't time to peel, prepare and cook other vegetables (though freshly prepared potatoes do taste better).
- **Tuna and salmon:** Great sandwich and microwaved jacket potato fillers or for adding to salad. Make quick fishcakes by mixing with leftover mashed potato and chopped fresh or frozen herbs.

## OILS AND VINEGARS

- **Olive oil:** For cooking and salad dressings.
- **Sesame oil:** Not an essential, but it does add a delicious flavour to many oriental dishes.
- **Sunflower, rapeseed or groundnut (peanut) oil:** For pan-frying and stir-fries.

## SPICES AND FLAVOUR ENHANCERS

- **Chinese five-spice:** A combination of spices that adds lots of taste to oriental dishes.
- **Dried chilli flakes:** A brilliant alternative to fresh chillies. Add a pinch or two to add heat and flavour to dishes.
- **Curry paste:** Much quicker and easier than using dried spices. Buy your favourite, whether mild, medium or hot.
- **Dried mixed herbs:** A good alternative to fresh in many dishes.
- **Garlic purée (paste):** A good substitute for fresh. 5 ml/1 tsp is the equivalent of one garlic clove.
- **Ginger:** Buy a bottle, tube or jar of grated root ginger or, if you prefer, buy fresh to peel and freeze when you have time; it is easy to grate from frozen.
- **Ground cumin and coriander:** Used in both Indian and North African dishes.
- **Ground turmeric:** Has a subtle flavour and brilliant yellow colour. Add a large pinch or two when cooking rice to accompany Indian dishes.
- **Mustard:** Have Dijon, wholegrain and English in the cupboard if you're a big mustard fan.
- **Salt and freshly ground black pepper:** Essential seasonings. Use a low-sodium salt if you prefer and take care not to over-season when there are other salty ingredients in the dish such as olives, anchovies, Feta cheese or soy sauce.
- **Soy sauce:** Gives a rich salty flavour to oriental food. The dark version is less salty than the light.
- **Stock cubes:** Good-quality vegetable, chicken and beef cubes or powdered bouillon, if you prefer. Vegetable stock cubes can be substituted for chicken and beef in most recipes if you want to buy only one type.

- **Sun-dried tomato purée (paste):** Richer than ordinary tomato purée as it has added garlic and herbs. Adds richness to soups, sauces and casseroles.
- **Thai fish sauce (nam pla):** For authentic Thai cuisine.
- **White wine vinegar and balsamic condiment:** Use as a basis for dressings and marinades.

## SWEET INGREDIENTS

- **Canned pineapple in natural juice fruit:** Good with meats such as pork and gammon, and sweet and sour dishes, or sprinkled with cinnamon sugar and grilled (broiled) for a quick dessert.
- **Dried fruit:** Apricots and raisins to add to salads, curries and rice dishes.
- **Jars of fruit compôte:** Can be folded into whipped cream or custard for instant fruit desserts or spooned on top of ice-cream, yoghurt or porridge.
- **Ratafia or amaretti biscuits (cookies):** Serve with coffee, broken and layered with fresh custard and fruit or soaked in sherry or other alcohol for a quick trifle base.
- **Sugar:** Caster (superfine), soft brown and icing (confectioners') sugar.
- **Vanilla essence (extract):** Adds a subtle, sophisticated flavour to many simple desserts.

## IN THE FRIDGE

- **Block of creamed coconut:** To add a wonderful creamy taste to curries and other dishes. Chop off what you need and quickly dissolve in boiling water to make coconut milk.
- **Bottled lemon juice:** Much quicker than squeezing a lemon.
- **Cheddar, Mozzarella and Parmesan cheeses:** Buy ready-grated to save time. Mature Cheddar has more flavour than mild, so less is needed in cooking.
- **Crème fraîche or double (heavy) cream:** Use in small quantities for rich sauces.
- **Eggs:** The ultimate fast food.
- **Greek-style yoghurt:** Good for dips and sauces and for an instant dessert drizzled with honey.
- **Mascarpone cheese:** Add a few spoonfuls to cooked pasta to create an instant sauce.
- **Milk:** Semi-skimmed.

## IN THE FREEZER

- **Berry fruits:** For special desserts (see pages 19–20).
- **Fish fillets:** Already skinned, such as haddock and tuna. If possible, defrost them in the fridge overnight.
- **Frozen chopped fresh herbs:** Keep a supply of those you use often, such as parsley and coriander (cilantro).

- **Frozen vegetables:** Such as peas, stir-fry vegetables, sliced mixed (bell) peppers and mushrooms.
- **Meat:** Including minced (ground) beef and chicken breasts. Buy packets of 'free-flow' loosely frozen mince as they take far less time to defrost (or may even be cooked from frozen) than blocks. Individually wrapped chicken breasts are particularly useful as you can easily remove and defrost the exact number needed. See also Top Tips for Making the Most of Your Freezer on pages 14–15.
- **Mixed seafood and cooked prawns (shrimp):** Can be added to stir-fries without defrosting.
- **Nuts:** Flaked (slivered) and ready toasted and chopped. Use from frozen in cooked dishes.
- **Ready-to-bake breads:** Such as ciabatta and foccacia.

# Equipment tips

You don't need lots of fancy equipment in the kitchen, but these are my favourite time-saving gadgets:

- A food processor speeds up chopping, mixing and puréeing, but washing-up takes longer! You are more likely to use it if you can keep it on your worktop rather than in a cupboard.
- A non-stick frying pan is essential for cooking with the minimum amount of fat without the food sticking.
- Pasta pans have an inner pot with small holes, which can simply be lifted out, making the pasta easy to drain without needing a colander.
- A pastry (paste) brush is useful for brushing marinades on to meat and for oiling the grill (broiler) pan to prevent food sticking.
- Ridged cast iron grill pans quickly seal and cook meat such as steak and chicken breasts, giving them an attractive striped brown finish and the appearance of barbecued food. It also allows any fat to drain away from the meat as it cooks.
- Scissors are handy for snipping fresh herbs and cutting the rinds off bacon rashers (slices).
- A timer is an essential piece of equipment. If you don't already have one on your oven, they are cheap to buy. Make sure it has a loud ring, or take it with you if you leave the kitchen.
- A zester lets you pare off narrow strips of citrus zest but leave the bitter pith.

# Fuss-free fast food

Ready-meals may seem like a good solution if you're short of time, but too often they are high in artificial additives, fat and salt and taste nothing like fresh food. In the following chapters you'll find lots of recipes that take around 15–20 minutes to prepare and cook; but sometimes you may want something even faster, so here are some simple suggestions.

## Perfect pasta

Most dried pastas cook in 10 minutes (wholemeal varieties take a little longer), but you can also buy quick-cook versions that take just 4–5 minutes. Cook the pasta in a large pan of boiling salted water (fill the pan with water boiled quickly in the kettle – put it on to boil as soon as you start preparation), allowing about 100 g/4 oz/1 cup of dried pasta shapes per person or a handful of spaghetti or other long pasta for a main course.

Keep a piece of fresh Parmesan cheese in your fridge to grate over the finished dish or buy ready-grated 'fresh' Parmesan (not the little tubs of powdery dry Parmesan, which have little flavour). In the following simple sauces, the quantities given are just a rough guide, so you don't have to waste time measuring and weighing.

- **Blue cheese:** Gently heat 175 g/6 oz/1½ cups of diced Gorgonzola and 40 g/1½ oz/3 tbsp of butter with 45 ml/3 tbsp of olive oil until melted. Stir in 45 ml/3 tbsp of single (light) cream.

- **Garlic mushrooms and bacon:** Fry a 100 g/4 oz packet of bacon lardons in a non-stick frying pan without added oil until lightly browned and crisp. Drain off the excess oil, then stir in 150 g/5 oz of chopped marinated wild mushrooms (from a jar) and a crushed smoked garlic clove. Cook for a few seconds, then stir in 45 ml/3 tbsp of Mascarpone or cream cheese and plenty of freshly ground black pepper. Heat gently until the cheese has just melted.

- **Herby tuna and sweetcorn:** Drain a 200 g/7 oz/small can of tuna in oil and a 200 g/7 oz/small can of sweetcorn. Put in a pan with 45 ml/3 tbsp of crème fraîche, 15 ml/1 tbsp of chopped fresh (or frozen) parsley and salt and pepper to taste. Heat very gently, stirring occasionally, until hot.

- **Roasted red (bell) pepper and pesto:** Roughly chop 225 g/8 oz of drained roasted red peppers (from a jar or the deli counter). Add to the drained pasta with 2–3 large spoonfuls of green pesto.

- **Spicy tomato:** Fry a crushed garlic clove or 5 ml/1 tsp of garlic purée in a little olive oil for a few seconds. Stir in a 400 g/14 oz/large can of chopped tomatoes with basil, 15 ml/1 tbsp of sun-dried tomato purée (paste) and a pinch of dried chilli flakes. Simmer gently for 3–4 minutes.

# Pizza panache

Why bother waiting for pizza delivery when you can create your own pizza with your favourite toppings in minutes? Supermarket pizzas may take only a few minutes to unwrap and pop in the oven, but the toppings are often scarce or unhealthy. Keep some ready-made frozen or long-life pizza bases, a jar of tomato-based pasta sauce or pesto in your fridge and some simple fresh ingredients and you'll soon be enjoying pizza as it should be. Before you start, turn on the oven to 200°C/400°F/gas 6/fan oven 180°C. Put a baking (cookie) sheet in the oven (this will help crisp the pizza base and catch any drips, which will help to keep the oven clean). Allow a 20–25 cm/8–10 in pizza base per person and spread it with 30–45 ml/2–3 tbsp of sauce or pesto. Scatter with one of the toppings below and cook for 12–15 minutes.

- **American hot:** Slices of pepperoni, jalapeño chillies (or stir a large pinch of dried chilli flakes into the pasta sauce before spreading over the pizza base) and ready-grated Mozzarella cheese.
- **Artichoke and mushroom:** Drained canned or bottled artichokes in oil, lightly sautéed sliced oyster mushrooms (cook them for a minute or two in a little of the oil from the artichokes), a few black olives, sliced Taleggio cheese and slivers of smoked garlic.
- **Chicken and blue cheese:** Shredded cooked chicken, cubed Gorgonzola cheese and pine nuts.
- **Marinara:** Antipasti-style marinated seafood and capers dotted with garlic- or herb-flavoured butter.
- **Mediterranean-style:** Green pesto, thinly sliced red onions tossed in olive oil, cubes of Feta cheese, black olives and anchovy fillets.
- **Mixed tomato and basil:** Spread the base with red pesto, top with sliced large tomatoes, sliced drained sun-dried tomatoes in oil and halved yellow cherry tomatoes and shavings of Parmesan (or use ready-grated). Scatter with basil leaves after baking.
- **Smoked salmon and dill:** Smoked salmon trimmings, dotted with a little Mascarpone cheese mixed with chopped fresh or frozen dill (dill weed) and freshly ground black pepper, scattered with grated or cubed Mozzarella cheese.

# Storage & freezing

As corner shops and supermarkets battle to have the longest opening hours, the idea of filling your storecupboard, fridge and freezer may seem a little outdated. It can, however, save both time and money in the long run.

## Storage times

Keep an eye on food labels. 'Best before' dates are used on less perishable foods such as dried pasta. The food may not taste quite as good but it will still be safe to eat a few weeks after the date has gone. 'Use by' dates mean what they say! They are found on fresh foods such as yoghurts and sliced meats. Once the date has passed, you can't be sure that the food is still safe to eat. When the outside of a food such as bread or a conserve goes mouldy, it's tempting to cut off or scrape away the mouldy bit and eat the rest; however, it's better to throw the whole thing away, as moulds and fungi have invisible toxins that can penetrate the entire food.

## Top tips for making the most of your fridge

- Keep an eye on the temperature of your fridge; it should be set at slightly below 40°F. The coldest part of the fridge is on the middle and top shelves; the least cold part is the door.
- Keep your fridge clean and wipe up spills as they occur; an antibacterial spray is ideal for this.
- Take care when storing uncooked meat and make sure it is well wrapped. Cooked meats should be kept above uncooked meat.
- Avoid storing strong-smelling foods such as raw onions, garlic or fish near eggs or opened milk, which will absorb their smell and flavour.
- Keep fruit and vegetables in the salad drawers or at the bottom of the fridge. Check them frequently as mould spreads quickly.

## Top tips for making the most of your freezer

- The freezer can be an invaluable asset for the busy cook. When you have time to spare, cook meals in bulk and freeze in family-sized or individual servings to eat later.
- When freezing chicken breasts, cut some into strips first for use in stir-fries and similar dishes; they'll defrost a lot quicker than whole chicken breasts.
- Buying loose minced (ground) meat should work out cheaper than buying ready-frozen, and you can also then freeze it in the exact amounts you need. Double wrap in non-PVC clingfilm (plastic wrap) and flatten thinly. This makes it easier to stack in the freezer and faster to defrost.
- Many of the recipes in this book suggest using fresh herbs. You can buy ready-prepared frozen chopped herbs; alternatively, prepare your own. Chop

the herbs and spoon into ice-cube trays. Pour just a little water into each, then freeze (you can transfer the cubes to plastic bags once they are solid). To use, defrost a cube or two on kitchen paper (paper towels); the water will be soaked up as it defrosts. Or you can add the frozen cube to hot sauces and stir-fries; it will quickly melt. Freezing works well for many herbs, including parsley, thyme and coriander (cilantro), but don't freeze tarragon or basil as they discolour.

- (Bell) peppers are often sold in packs of three or more. If you are unlikely to use them all within a few days, prepare and slice or dice the excess and freeze. Although they won't be suitable for cold dishes or salads, they are still great for adding to cooked dishes like stir-fries.

- Label and date containers clearly; it's easy to forget what you've frozen and find you've thawed apple purée when you wanted soup! Labelling with a 'use by' date is more helpful than the date on which the food was frozen (see the chart below).

- Thawing must be thorough (especially poultry) to ensure the food is safe to eat – the best place is overnight in the fridge. Do not refreeze food once it has thawed.

- Keep a supply of standby foods in the freezer, so there's always something to hand when the shops are closed or you've been away for a few days. A loaf of bread (slices can be toasted from frozen) and a carton (not glass bottle) of milk (defrost overnight for breakfast) are always useful.

- Some foods do not freeze well. These include cream (although whipped double (heavy) cream is fine), yoghurt and mayonnaise, jellies (jello) and foods containing gelatine, hard-boiled (hard-cooked) eggs and watery vegetables such as lettuce and cucumber.

# Quick guide to freezer storage times

| 1 month | Unblanched vegetables |
|---|---|
| 2 months | Sausages |
| 3 months | Bread, sandwiches, pastries and cakes<br>Butter and soft cheeses<br>Minced (ground) meats such as beef<br>Shellfish<br>Soups and sauces |
| 4 months | Beef, lamb, pork, chicken and turkey<br>Hard cheeses<br>Oily fish<br>Prepared meals |
| 5 months | Whipped double (heavy) cream |
| 6 months | White fish<br>Open-frozen fruit and fruit purées |
| 10 months | Blanched vegetables |

# Planning ahead

The recipes in this book enable you to produce delicious meals as quickly and easily as possible. It's important to get organised, so list all the ingredients you need and buy the fresh ones on or as near to the day you intend to cook them as possible, so that they remain in peak condition. If, like many people, you do your main food shopping at the weekend, serve meals made with fresh vegetables and salad ingredients early in the week; later in the week you can rely more on frozen and canned vegetables, meats and seafood from the freezer (remember to defrost in the fridge overnight), dried pasta and grains.

Pre-washed and cut vegetables are more expensive to buy, but they reduce preparation time considerably, as does buying ready-trimmed meat and skinned and filleted fish – get to know your butcher and fishmonger because their help and advice can be invaluable. If you plan your weekly menu in advance (see below), internet shopping with delivery to your door is a great timesaver.

Try to find a few minutes each week to plan the meals you're going to eat over the next seven days. It will save you time and energy in the long run as you won't have to dash out to the corner shop (or resort to having a takeaway) because your fridge is bare. Below are menu suggestions and shopping lists for four weeks to get you started.

## Four-week main-meal planner

### ■ WEEK 1

Monday      Chicken, mushroom and spinach lasagne (see page 50)
Tuesday     Fruity beef salad with mustard and ginger dressing (see page 66)
Wednesday   Boston beans and vegetables (see page 124)
Thursday    Spicy pork and apricot curry (see page 77)
Friday      Oriental fish parcels (see page 94)
Saturday    Turkey and mixed vegetable frittata (see page 61)
Sunday      Lamb noisettes with an almond and lemon crust (see page 82)

*Check in the storecupboard/fridge for:*
Canned baked beans, canned red kidney beans, canned chopped tomatoes, passata (sieved tomatoes), vegetable stock cubes, ready-to-eat dried apricots, olive oil, sunflower oil, sesame oil, hazelnut (filbert) or walnut oil, butter, cornflour (cornstarch), chilli powder or dried chilli flakes, cumin seeds, ground paprika, dried mixed herbs, nutmeg, Dijon or wholegrain mustard, white wine vinegar, cider, dark brown sugar, black treacle (molasses), soy sauce, flaked (slivered) almonds, rice (cellophane) noodles or egg noodles, rice, mini popadoms.

*Check in the freezer for:*
Mixed vegetables.

*Shopping list:*
**Dairy:** Milk, 150 ml/¼ pint/⅔ cup single (light) cream, ready-grated Parmesan cheese, 6 eggs.
**Meat and fish:** 4 skinless, boneless chicken breasts, 350 g/12 oz ready-cooked turkey, 2 thick-cut sirloin steaks, 400 g/14 oz pork tenderloin, 4 white fish portions, 8 small lamb noisettes.

**Fruit and vegetables:** 1 lemon, 100 g/4 oz red grapes, 175 g/6 oz chestnut button mushrooms, 100 g/4 oz oyster mushrooms, fresh garlic (or garlic purée), 175 g/6 oz young leaf spinach, greens, courgettes (zucchini) or green beans, 150 g/5 oz/2½ cups beansprouts, a 100 g/4 oz bag of herb or baby salad leaves, fresh root ginger (or bottled grated root ginger), 2 red chillies (or dried chilli flakes), 3 onions, celery, new potatoes, roasting or baking potatoes, 1 red and 1 green (bell) pepper, a 300 g/11 oz packet of stir-fry vegetables, fresh (or frozen chopped) coriander (cilantro), fresh (or frozen chopped) parsley, rosemary.
**Other:** Fresh lasagne, crusty French bread.

## WEEK 2

Monday        Chilli corned beef with noodles (see page 65)
Tuesday       Roasted vegetable salad with Feta cheese and polenta (see page 123)
Wednesday  Spicy coconut chicken (see page 45)
Thursday      Cantonese sweet and sour beef (see page 70)
Friday           Smoked haddock and summer vegetables (see page 101)
Saturday      Easy chicken tikka masala (see page 49)
Sunday         Rosemary lamb and potato kebabs (see page 81)

### Check in the storecupboard/fridge for:
Canned corned beef, canned tomatoes, canned coconut milk, canned pineapple rings, canned new potatoes, olive oil, sunflower oil, soy sauce, hoisin sauce, sweet chilli sauce, red curry paste, garam masala, ground turmeric, ground paprika, balsamic condiment, lemon juice, cornflour (cornstarch), caster (superfine) sugar, dry sherry, red wine vinegar, egg noodles, rice.

### Shopping list:
**Dairy:** Feta cheese, crème fraîche, 150 ml/¼ pint/⅔ cup soured (dairy sour) cream, 150 ml/¼ pint/⅔ cup double (heavy) cream.
**Meat and fish:** 3 skinless, boneless chicken breasts, 2 rump steaks, 450 g/1 lb lamb neck fillet, 4 smoked haddock pieces, two 200 g/7 oz packets of ready-cooked tikka chicken breast pieces.
**Fruit and vegetables:** 2 onions, fresh garlic (or garlic purée), 10 spring onions (scallions), 1 lemon (or bottled lemon juice) 2 tomatoes, 250 g/9 oz baby plum tomatoes, 16 cherry tomatoes, fresh root ginger (or bottled grated root ginger), 200 g/7 oz mushrooms, 200 g/7 oz green beans, 4 courgettes (zucchini), 12 baby new potatoes, 1 carrot, 50 g/2 oz beansprouts, 1 red, 1 yellow and 2 green (bell) peppers, red and green chillies, rocket (arugula) leaves, 100 g/4 oz asparagus tips, fresh (or frozen chopped) coriander (cilantro), fresh chives, fresh rosemary, fresh mint.
**Other:** Instant polenta, popadoms, naan breads.

## WEEK 3

Monday        Easy vegetable lasagne (see page 112)
Tuesday       Hoisin pork skewers (see page 78)
Wednesday  Chicken salad niçoise (see page 53)
Thursday      Quick Quorn burgers (see page 119)
Friday           Warm salmon and bean salad with Parmesan croûtons (see page 102)
Saturday      Spiced minced beef and pea curry (see page 73)
Sunday         Creamy turkey and mushroom stroganoff (see page 57)

### Check in the storecupboard/fridge for:
Canned ratatouille, canned anchovies, hoisin sauce, stir-fry rice noodles, olive oil, sunflower oil, Dijon mustard, ground paprika, plain (all-purpose) flour, butter or sunflower margarine, black olives, bottled lemon juice, red pesto sauce, tomato relish or ketchup (catsup), curry paste, ranch-style dressing, chicken stock cubes, beef or vegetable stock cubes, nutmeg, ground paprika, brown or white rice.

**Check in the freezer for:**
Frozen peas, oven chips.

**Shopping list:**
**Dairy:** Milk, 100 g/4 oz ready-grated Mozzarella or Cheddar cheese, ready-grated Parmesan cheese, crème fraîche, 4 eggs, thick plain yoghurt.
**Meat and fish:** 450 g/1 lb lean pork, 400 g/14 oz lean minced (ground) beef, 350 g/ 12 oz turkey breast steaks, 3 cooked chicken breasts, 4 salmon fillets.
**Fruit and vegetables:** 1 large red (bell) pepper, 100 g/4 oz mangetout (snow peas), 200 g/7 oz button mushrooms, 250 g/9 oz large chestnut mushrooms, 2 lemons (for the juice, or bottled lemon juice), 400 g/14 oz fine green beans, runner beans, courgettes (zucchini), 6 Little Gem lettuces, lettuce leaves, 2 tomatoes, cherry tomatoes, 1 cucumber, 2 onions, 2 red onions, 100 g/4 oz potatoes, fresh garlic (or garlic purée), fresh (or frozen chopped) parsley, fresh basil, fresh mint.
**Other:** Fresh lasagne, a 350 g/12 oz pack of minced (ground) Quorn, bread for breadcrumbs, 4 burger baps, ciabatta, garlic or plain foccacia, naan bread, popadoms, coleslaw.

## ■ WEEK 4

Monday       Mediterranean vegetable pasta (see page 115)
Tuesday      Chicken and tropical fruit kebabs with couscous (see page 54)
Wednesday    Beef and mushroom sauté (see page 69)
Thursday     Lamb and vegetable pilaff (see page 85)
Friday       Fish fingers and bean pitta pockets (see page 89)
Saturday     Mixed vegetable stir-fry with teriyaki tofu (page 120)
Sunday       Italian turkey escalopes (see page 58)

**Check in the storecupboard/fridge for:**
Canned borlotti or cannellini beans, canned pineapple chunks, olive oil, sunflower oil, sesame oil, soy sauce, sweet chilli sauce, mirin or dry sherry, Marsala or Madeira, clear honey, chicken stock cubes, vegetable stock cubes, plain (all-purpose) flour, basmati or long-grain rice, couscous, ground turmeric, Chinese five-spice powder, egg noodles, oyster sauce, curry paste, mayonnaise, black olives, egg noodles.

**Check in the freezer for:**
Mixed vegetables, fish fingers.

**Shopping list:**
**Dairy:** 4 eggs.
**Meat and fish:** 4 skinless, boneless chicken breasts, 4 turkey breast steaks, 400 g/14 oz rump steak, 400 g/14 oz lean minced (ground) lamb, 4 slices of Parma ham.
**Fruit and vegetables:** 1 lemon, 2 limes, 2 oranges, 1 mango, a 300 g/11 oz packet of stir-fry vegetables, 1 aubergine (eggplant), potatoes for sautéing, 1 red onion, courgettes (zucchini), 2 red (bell) peppers, green and red chillies, 2 Little Gem lettuces, 100 g/4 oz shiitake or chestnut mushrooms, 200 g/7 oz broccoli florets, fresh garlic (or garlic purée), fresh root ginger (or bottled grated root ginger), fresh mint, fresh (or frozen chopped) parsley, fresh (or frozen chopped) coriander (cilantro), fresh basil.
**Other:** a 275 g/10 oz packet of tofu, a 500 g/18 oz packet of stuffed pasta, fresh roasted vegetable pasta sauce or tomato pasta sauce, 4 pitta breads, crusty French or country-style bread.

# Super-quick sweets

Most evenings, some seasonal fresh fruit or yoghurt will be all you need to finish off your meal, but sometimes you may be entertaining or simply want something a little more special. These speedy desserts, all of which make four servings, are the solution.

## Hot puddings

### QUICK CRUMBLE

Drain most of the juice from a 400 g/14 oz/large can or jar of pear or apple halves or peach slices, then tip the fruit and a little of the juice or syrup into an ovenproof dish. For the topping, put 50 g/2 oz/½ cup of wholemeal flour, 50 g/2 oz/½ cup of porridge oats and 15 ml/1 tbsp of light brown sugar into a bowl and stir together. Drizzle with 30 ml/2 tbsp of sunflower oil and stir until mixed. Sprinkle the topping over the fruit and bake at 190°C/375°F/gas 5/fan oven 170°C for 15–20 minutes. You need not waste the remaining fruit juice either: Blend 5 ml/1 tsp of cornflour (cornstarch) with a little of the juice in a small pan. Stir in the rest of the juice, bring to the boil and simmer for a minute until thickened. Serve as a sauce with the crumble.

### HOT CHOCOLATE POTS

Put 1 egg, 40 g/1½ oz of cocoa (unsweetened chocolate) powder, 40 g/1½ oz of caster (superfine) sugar, 50 g/2 oz/¼ cup of softened unsalted (sweet) butter and 5 ml/1 tsp of vanilla essence (extract) in a food processor. Blend until smooth. Bring 75 ml/5 tbsp of whole milk to the boil in a small pan, then add to the food processor and blend on a high speed until smooth. Pour into espresso coffee cups and serve straight away. These are also good chilled in the fridge for several hours and served cold.

### SPEEDY GINGER SPONGE

Spoon 2 pieces of chopped preserved ginger and 45 ml/3 tbsp of ginger syrup from the jar into a well-buttered baking dish. Sift 50 g/2 oz/½ cup of self-raising flour and 5 ml/1 tsp of ground ginger into a bowl. Add 50 g/2 oz/¼ cup of light brown sugar, 50 g/2 oz/¼ cup of soft margarine or softened butter and 1 lightly beaten egg. Beat everything together until light and smooth, then spoon into the prepared dish. Bake at 180°C/350°F/gas 4/fan oven 160°C for 15–20 minutes. If you prefer to use the microwave, cook on High for about 3 minutes. Serve with bought custard or cream.

### ICY BERRIES WITH WARM WHITE CHOCOLATE SAUCE

Divide a 450 g/1 lb bag of frozen mixed summer berries (such as raspberries, strawberries, blueberries and blackcurrants) between four small plates. If time allows, let them defrost for about 5 minutes. Put 150 g/5 oz/1¼ cups of white chocolate drops in a heatproof bowl. Add 150 ml/¼ pint/⅔ cup of single (light) cream and 5 ml/1 tsp of clear honey. Place the bowl over a pan of gently simmering water and stir until the chocolate has melted and you have a smooth sauce. Drizzle the sauce over the berries and serve straight away.

### PEAR AND CINNAMON TARTS

Drain a 400 g/14 oz/large can of pear halves. Select the four largest and pat dry on kitchen paper (paper towels). Cut a sheet of ready-rolled puff pastry (paste) into four squares and place them on a baking (cookie) sheet. Lightly brush with milk. Top each

with a pear half, cut-side down. Mix 30 ml/2 tbsp of caster (superfine) sugar with 5 ml/ 1 tsp of ground cinnamon and sprinkle over the pears and pastry. Bake in a preheated oven at 220°C/425°F/gas 7/fan oven 200°C for 20 minutes or until the pastry is golden-brown and crisp. Serve with crème fraîche or ice-cream.

### SPICED RICE

Put 75 g/3 oz of flaked rice, 25 g/1 oz/2 tbsp of light brown sugar and 750 ml/ 1¼ pints/3 cups of semi-skimmed milk in a heavy-based saucepan. Add a cinnamon stick and bring to the boil. Simmer for 12 minutes or until cooked and thickened. Remove the cinnamon stick (rinse and air-dry to use another time). Grate a little nutmeg over and serve topped with fresh or soaked dried fruit.

# Cold desserts

### APRICOT FOOL

Mix 450 g/1 lb of bottled apricot compôte with 150 ml/¼ pint/⅔ cup of ready-made fresh custard and 150 ml/¼ pint/⅔ cup of plain yoghurt. Spoon into glasses and serve decorated with ready-toasted flaked (slivered) almonds.

### LUSCIOUS LEMON TARTS

Fold together equal quantities of lemon curd and whipped cream. Use to fill bought sweet mini pastry (paste) cases or brandy snap baskets.

### CHEAT'S CRÈME BRULÉE

Blend 150 g/5 oz/⅔ cup of Mascarpone cheese with 25 g/1 oz/2 tbsp of caster (superfine) sugar. Stir in a 250 g/9 oz carton of fresh custard and a 100 g/4 oz pot of crème fraîche. Divide between four ramekin dishes (custard cups) and chill in the fridge for 2 hours or in the freezer for 10 minutes. Generously sprinkle with caster sugar and put under a hot grill (broiler) for 2–3 minutes until caramelised. Serve straight away.

### RAPID RASPBERRY CRUSH

Lightly mash 150 g/5 oz of fresh raspberries with 5 ml/1 tsp of caster (superfine) sugar in a bowl. Add 50 g/2 oz of meringues broken into chunks and 150 ml/¼ pint/⅔ cup of Greek-style yoghurt. Spoon into sundae glasses and decorate the tops with a few whole fresh raspberries.

### MANGO AND LIME SYLLABUB

Peel and roughly chop the flesh of 2 ripe mangoes. Put in a food processor and blend until smooth. Mix together the grated zest and juice of 1 lime with 30 ml/2 tbsp of Malibu or brandy and 30 ml/2 tbsp of icing (confectioners') sugar in a bowl. Add 150 ml/¼ pint/⅔ cup of whipping cream and whisk until it forms soft peaks. Stir in the mango purée and divide between four glasses. Chill until ready to serve.

# Notes on the recipes

- Do not mix metric, imperial and American measures. Follow one set only.

- American terms are given in brackets.

- The ingredients are listed in the order in which they are used in the recipe.

- All spoon measurements are level: 1 tsp=5ml; 1 tbsp=15 ml.

- Eggs are medium unless otherwise stated. If you use a different size, you may need to adjust the amount of liquid added to obtain the right consistency.

- Always wash, peel, core and seed, if necessary, fresh foods before use. Ensure that all produce is as fresh as possible and in good condition.

- The use of strongly flavoured ingredients such as garlic, chilli and ginger depends on personal taste and quantities can be adjusted accordingly.

- Preparation and cooking times are approximate and are intended as a guide only. The time it takes for food to cook will depend on personal preference and your oven.

- The can and packet sizes given are approximate and will depend on the particular brand.

- Vegetarian recipes are marked with a V symbol. Those who eat fish but not meat will find plenty of additional recipes containing seafood to enjoy. Some vegetarian recipes contain dairy products, so you should check packets to make sure you buy acceptable versions. Recipes may also use processed foods and vegetarians should check the specific product labels to be certain of their suitability, especially items such as breads and stock cubes.

# snacks
# &
# light meals

All the recipes in this book are quick and easy to prepare and cook, but in this chapter you'll find some of the fastest and simplest ones, designed for those days when you've already had a main meal or just want a light lunch or supper dish.

You'll find a wide choice here to suit all tastes; familiar dishes such as Easy Cheese, Ham and Tomato Pizza and traditional ones with a twist, including Prawn Cocktail with Eggs and Avocado. Some, such as Pastrami and Cream Cheese Wrap with Roast Onion, are ideal for packed lunches and picnics. For vegetarians, Polenta with Asparagus and Melting Mozzarella is a delicious choice.

This chapter makes the most of ingredients from the delicatessen shop or counter, such as smoked trout or salmon, pastrami, Parma ham and ready-made polenta and pancakes and shows you how to combine them with a few ingredients to make super-quick meals.

# Prawn and chicken kebabs
## with mixed pepper couscous

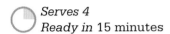

*Serves 4*
*Ready in* 15 minutes

4 skinless, boneless chicken breasts, cubed

24 shelled raw tiger prawns (shrimp)

15 ml/1 tbsp olive oil

Finely grated zest and juice of 1 lime

5 ml/1 tsp fresh thyme leaves or 2.5 ml/½ tsp dried

Salt and freshly ground black pepper

1 lemon, cut into wedges

1 lime, cut into wedges

*For the couscous:*

400 ml/14 fl oz/1¾ cups hot vegetable stock or water

250 g/9 oz/1½ cups couscous

275 g/10 oz jar of mixed roasted peppers in oil, drained and chopped

30 ml/2 tbsp chopped fresh or frozen parsley

**1** Place the chicken, prawns, oil, lime zest and juice, thyme and seasoning in a bowl and mix together. If you have time, leave to marinade for 5 minutes to let the flavours mingle. Thread the chicken, prawns and lemon and lime wedges on to skewers.

**2** Heat a large ridged cast iron grill (broiler) pan or non-stick frying pan until hot. Place the kebabs in the pan and cook for 4–5 minutes, then turn and cook for a further 4–5 minutes until lightly charred and cooked through.

**3** Meanwhile, to make the couscous, pour the stock or water into a saucepan (add a pinch of salt if using water) and bring to the boil. Pour in the couscous in a steady stream and stir thoroughly. Turn off the heat, cover the pan with a tight-fitting lid to retain the steam and leave to stand for 5 minutes.

**4** Add the chopped peppers to the couscous and heat gently for 2 minutes, stirring and separating the grains with a fork. Pile the couscous on to four serving plates and top with the kebabs. Garnish with the parsley and serve.

## Tip

★ If using wooden or bamboo kebab skewers, soak them in cold water for a few minutes while preparing the ingredients; this helps stop them charring and prevents them soaking up the juices from the chicken.

# Prawn cocktail
## with eggs and avocado

*Serves 4*
*Ready in* 15 minutes

4 eggs

½ Iceberg lettuce, finely shredded

250 g/9 oz cooked, peeled prawns (shrimp)

2 ripe avocadoes, peeled and sliced

5 ml/1 tsp freshly squeezed or bottled lemon juice

5 ml/1 tsp tomato purée (paste)

10 ml/2 tsp cold water

30 ml/2 tbsp mayonnaise

15 ml/1 tbsp Greek-style yoghurt or crème fraîche

Salt and freshly ground black pepper

**1** Put the eggs in a pan and cover them with tepid water. Heat the water until bubbling gently, then simmer for 8 minutes. Remove from the pan with a slotted spoon and place in a bowl of cold water. When cool enough to handle, peel off the shells and halve the eggs lengthways.

**2** Divide the lettuce between four small bowls or glasses and top with the prawns, avocado slices and hard-boiled (hard-cooked) egg halves.

**3** Blend together the lemon juice, tomato purée and water in a small bowl. Add the mayonnaise, yoghurt or crème fraîche and a pinch of salt and stir until mixed. Drizzle the dressing over the salad. Grind a little black pepper over and serve straight away.

*Serve with:* Thin slices of buttered brown bread or lightly toasted slices of ciabatta or French bread

## Tips

★ When cooking chilled eggs straight from the fridge, it is best to put them into cold or tepid water or they may crack. If you keep your eggs at room temperature, or have remembered to take them out of the fridge an hour before starting to cook, you can lower them on a spoon straight into simmering water.

★ Instead of making the above dressing, you could use 60 ml/4 tbsp of bought thousand island dressing.

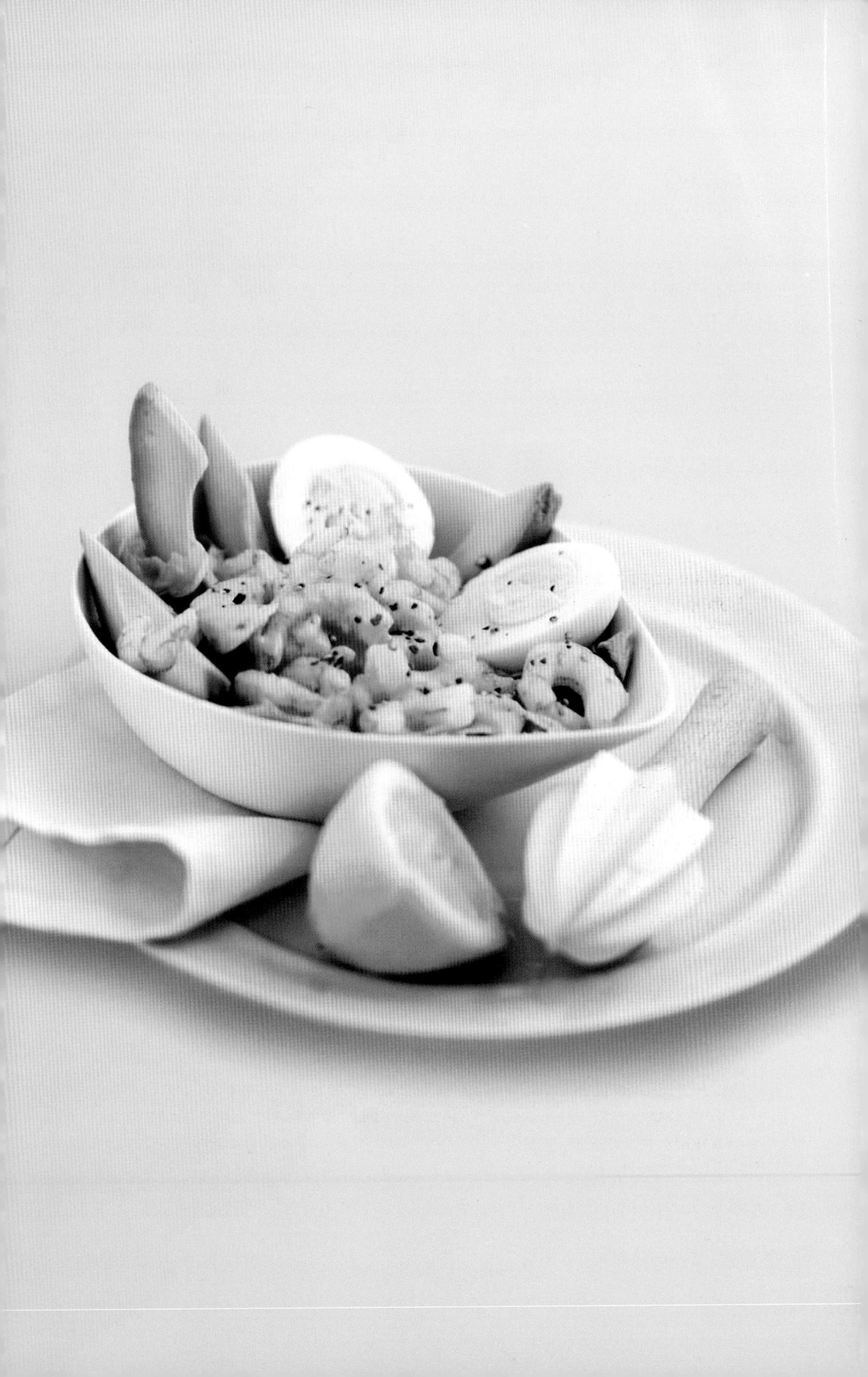

# Smoked salmon
## and new potato salad

*Serves 4*
*Ready in* 20 minutes

400 g/14 oz even-sized new potatoes, quartered

10 ml/2 tsp creamed horseradish sauce

30 ml/2 tbsp sunflower oil

10 ml/2 tsp freshly squeezed or bottled lemon juice

Salt and freshly ground black pepper

A 100 g/4 oz bag of mixed salad leaves or 1 small head of radicchio and 1 Little Gem lettuce, sliced

1 ripe avocado, peeled and diced

100 g/4 oz smoked salmon, cut into thin strips

1   Boil the potatoes in lightly salted water for 15 minutes or until tender.

2   Meanwhile, make the dressing by whisking together the horseradish sauce, oil, lemon juice and seasoning in a small bowl with a fork, or by shaking them together in a screw-topped jar.

3   Drain the potatoes in a colander. Briefly rinse with cold water to stop them cooking further, then drain again. Tip the potatoes into a bowl, drizzle with half the dressing and toss together to coat.

4   Divide the salad leaves between four bowls or plates. Top with the potatoes, diced avocado and salmon strips. Drizzle the remaining dressing over and serve straight away.

*Serve with:* Crusty white rolls or wholemeal French bread

## Tips

★   If preferred, use 45 ml/3 tbsp of bought French dressing instead of the horseradish dressing.

★   Smoked salmon trimmings are ideal for this dish as they add a luxurious touch but are less expensive than smoked salmon slices.

# Herb omelette
## with smoked trout

*Serves 4*
*Ready in* 15 minutes

5 large eggs

45 ml/3 tbsp chopped fresh or frozen herbs such as dill (dill weed), parsley and chervil

30 ml/2 tbsp cold water

Salt and freshly ground black pepper

25 g/1 oz/2 tbsp unsalted (sweet) butter

5 ml/1 tsp olive oil

175 g/6 oz smoked trout, cut into thin strips

*For the dressing:*

120 ml/4 fl oz/½ cup fromage frais or Greek-style yoghurt

15 ml/1 tbsp fresh or bottled lemon juice

10 ml/2 tsp white wine vinegar

A pinch of caster (superfine) sugar

1    Crack the eggs into a bowl, then add the herbs, water and a little salt and pepper. Beat just enough to break up the eggs; take care not to overbeat, as this will spoil the texture of the omelette.

2    Heat the butter and oil in a large non-stick frying pan until melted. Pour in the egg mixture and cook for about 1 minute, stirring gently. When the omelette begins to set, stop stirring and cook for about 2 minutes or until the base is set. Flip over and cook the other side until golden.

3    While the omelette is cooking, make the dressing. Put all the ingredients in a bowl, adding salt and pepper to taste, and stir together until evenly blended. Taste and add more lemon juice or sugar, if necessary.

4    Cut the omelette into wedges and serve straight away topped with strips of smoked trout and a drizzle of the dressing.

*Serve with:* Wedges of lemon and sprigs of fresh dill to garnish (optional)

## Tips

★   You can omit the herbs and use gravadlax instead of smoked trout.

★   Instead of turning the omelette in the pan, you can brown the top under a preheated hot grill (broiler) for 2–3 minutes.

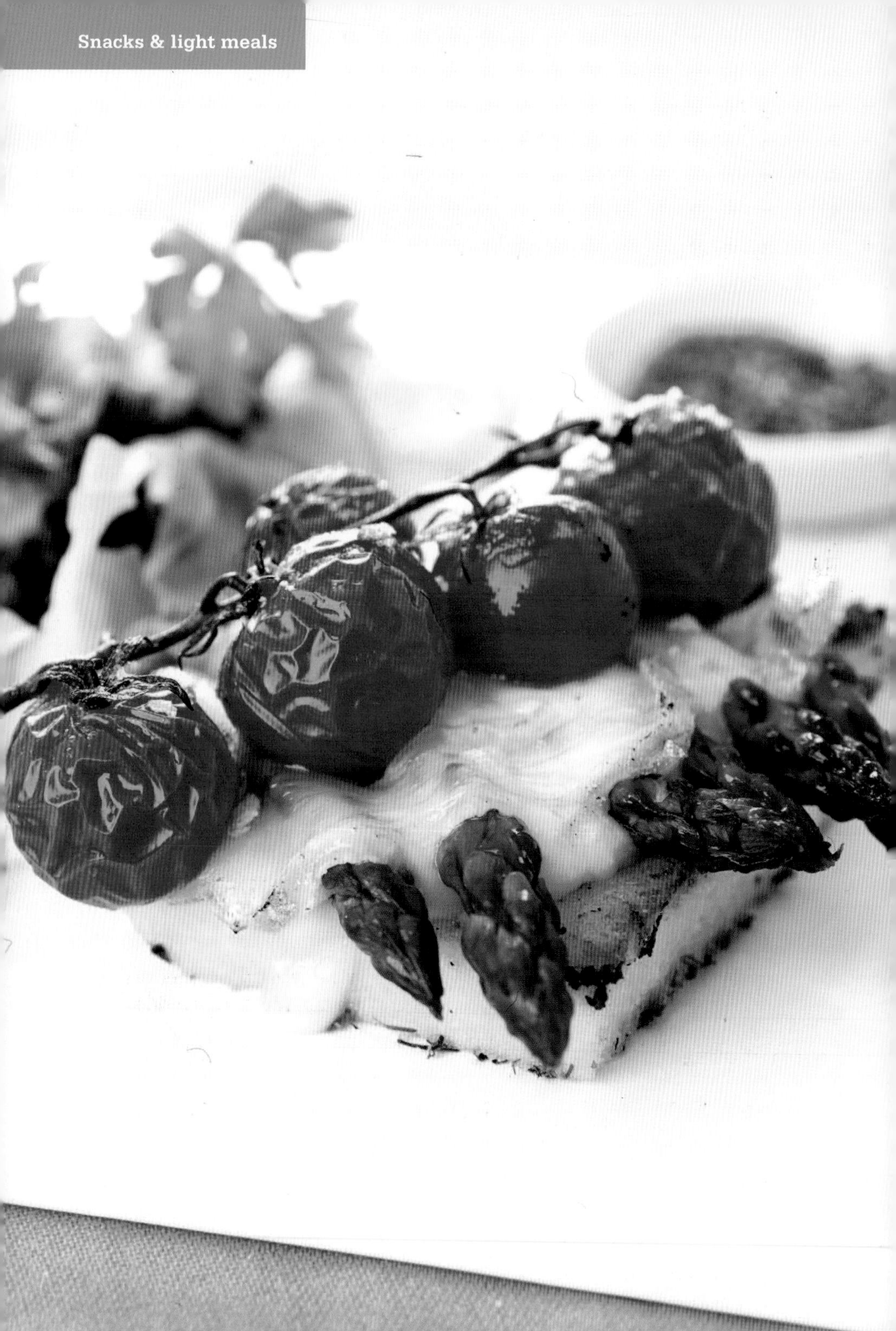

# Polenta with asparagus
## and melting Mozzarella   V

*Serves 4*
*Ready in* 15 minutes

A 500 g/18 oz block of polenta
2.5 ml/½ tsp dried mixed herbs
Salt and freshly ground black pepper
30 ml/2 tbsp olive oil
225 g/8 oz cherry tomatoes on the vine
A pinch of caster (superfine) sugar
225 g/8 oz asparagus tips
175 g/6 oz Mozzarella cheese, thinly sliced

1   Slice the polenta in half horizontally, then halve each piece again to give four squares. Sprinkle the herbs and a little salt and pepper over.

2   Heat half the oil in a large non-stick frying pan, add the polenta and fry for 2–3 minutes on each side until golden and crisp.

3   Meanwhile, preheat the grill (broiler) to moderately hot. Place the tomatoes, still on the vine, in a roasting tin and drizzle with the remaining oil, then sprinkle with the sugar. Cook under the grill for 4–5 minutes until the skins begin to split.

4   Cook the asparagus tips in boiling lightly salted water for about 3 minutes or until just tender (test by piercing a stalk with a thin sharp knife – it should slide in easily). Drain thoroughly.

5   Pile the asparagus tips on top of the polenta, then cover with the Mozzarella slices. Pop under the grill for 1–2 minutes until the cheese is bubbling, then serve straight away with the vine tomatoes to one side.

*Serve with:* Mixed salad leaves

## Tip

★   To save time, or if fresh asparagus is out of season or unavailable, use canned asparagus tips instead. Tip them with their liquid into a saucepan and heat until piping hot. Drain thoroughly before using.

# Garlic mushroom cheeseburger

**Serves 4**
**Ready in** 15 minutes

4 large flat mushrooms
15 ml/1 tbsp olive oil
15 g/½ oz/1 tbsp butter, diced
2 garlic cloves, peeled and thinly sliced, or 10 ml/2 tsp garlic purée (paste)
4 fresh or frozen burgers
4 cheese slices

**1** Preheat the grill (broiler) to medium. Line the grill pan with foil. Trim the mushroom stalks, then place the mushrooms on one side of the grill pan, stalk-side down. Brush the mushroom tops with the oil.

**2** Grill (broil) the mushrooms for 7–8 minutes or until the juices start to run. Turn them over and dot with the butter and sprinkle with the garlic. Grill for a further 5–7 minutes, basting with the juices, until tender.

**3** At the same time as the mushrooms are cooking, place the burgers on the other side of the pan and cook according to the packet instructions, turning once, until well browned and cooked through.

**4** Place the burgers on individual plates and top each with a cheese slice and a garlic mushroom. Serve straight away while hot, as the cheese starts to melt.

*Serve with:* Toasted burger buns or sliced ciabatta, quartered tomatoes and mixed salad leaves

## Tip

★ Check out the fresh meat counter for a wide range of tasty burgers, often with added flavourings such as fresh herbs or chillies. Look out for those made with lean minced (ground) steak, lamb and chicken burgers. For vegetarians, serve bean or Quorn burgers.

# Pastrami and cream cheese wrap with roasted onion

*Serves 4*
*Ready in* 15 minutes

2 onions, peeled and each cut into 8 wedges
15 ml/1 tbsp olive oil
Salt and freshly ground black pepper
4 x 20 cm/8 in soft flour tortillas
200 g/7 oz/scant 1 cup soft cream cheese
50 g/2 oz rocket (arugula) leaves
16 slices of pastrami

**1** Preheat the grill (broiler) to moderately hot. Toss the onion wedges in the oil and arrange on a baking tray. Sprinkle with a little salt and pepper and cook under the grill for 8–10 minutes, turning half-way through, until the onions are soft and lightly charred. Tip into a bowl and leave to cool for a few minutes.

**2** Meanwhile, stack the tortillas and place on a heatproof plate. Microwave on High for 1 minute. Spread each tortilla thickly with cream cheese, top with roasted onions, then scatter a few rocket leaves down the centre. Top each with 4 slices of pastrami.

**3** Tuck in the sides of each tortilla, then roll up to enclose the filling. Cut in half and serve straight away while the onions are still slightly warm.

*Serve with:* Guacamole or houmous to spoon on top

## Tips

★ Microwaving the tortillas not only warms them but also makes them more flexible and easier to roll. If you prefer them lightly browned, warm them in a frying pan over a moderate heat for about 45 seconds on each side.

★ Tortillas usually come in packs of six or eight. Re-seal the bag and pop the remaining ones in the freezer for another time.

# Easy cheese, ham and tomato pizza

*Serves 4*
*Ready in* 20 minutes

4 individual pizza bases, each about 20 cm/8 in in diameter

250 g/9 oz Mozzarella cheese, drained and sliced

16 baby plum tomatoes, halved lengthways

16 slices of Parma ham

15 ml/1 tbsp olive oil

Freshly ground black pepper

50 g/2 oz wild rocket (arugula) leaves

**1** Put two baking (cookie) sheets in the oven on the top and middle shelves and preheat to 220°C/425°F/gas 7/fan oven 200°C.

**2** Unwrap the pizza bases and arrange the Mozzarella slices, tomato halves and Parma ham on top. Drizzle lightly with the oil.

**3** Place the pizzas on the hot baking sheets and bake for 10 minutes or until the cheese is bubbling and beginning to brown. Remove from the oven, grind a little black pepper over and scatter the rocket leaves over. Serve straight away.

*Serve with:* Bought or home-made coleslaw

## Tips

* Ready-made pizza bases are an excellent standby. Most have a long shelf-life or can be kept in the freezer for a month or two. They are delicious with a huge variety of toppings. Try spreading them with a little sun-dried tomato purée (paste), then topping with sliced pepperoni, quartered mushrooms and Mozzarella slices, or tuna and sweetcorn and grated Cheddar cheese.

* Save time by using ready-grated Mozzarella or mini Mozzarella balls.

* The baking sheets will catch any drips from the pizzas and save you cleaning the oven but, if you prefer, the pizzas can be cooked directly on the oven shelves.

# Ratatouille and chicken salad pancakes

*Serves 4*
*Ready in* 20 minutes

15 ml/1 tbsp olive oil

1 onion, finely chopped

1 garlic clove, crushed, or 5 ml/1 tsp garlic purée (paste)

1 red (bell) pepper, seeded and roughly diced

1 yellow pepper, seeded and roughly diced

100 g/4 oz aubergine (eggplant), cut into cubes

400 g/14 oz/large can of cherry tomatoes in juice

60 ml/4 tbsp mixed fresh or frozen chopped herbs such as basil, parsley and chives

Salt and freshly ground black pepper

4 bought unsweetened pancakes or crêpes

A 200 g/7 oz bag of mixed salad leaves

3 cooked chicken breasts, shredded

1   Heat the oil in a large non-stick pan, add the onion and cook over a medium heat for 3–4 minutes until beginning to soften.

2   Add the garlic, chopped peppers and aubergine and cook for a further 3 minutes, stirring frequently.

3   Stir in the tomatoes and their juice and bring the mixture to the boil. Simmer, uncovered, for 5 minutes or until the vegetables are very tender and the liquid has reduced to a fairly thick sauce.

4   Remove the ratatouille mixture from the heat and stir in the herbs. Season with salt and pepper to taste.

5   Lay the pancakes or crêpes on a clean surface and divide the salad leaves down the centre of each. Top with the ratatouille mixture and shredded chicken. Roll up each pancake to enclose the filling, cut in half and serve straight away.

## Tips

★   You can buy jars of garlic purée in the supermarket. It's especially good for those recipes when you only want a small amount of garlic and once opened will keep in the fridge for a couple of months.

★   If you can't find canned cherry tomatoes, use a can of chopped tomatoes instead.

# chicken & turkey

For succulence, flavour and versatility, chicken and turkey are hard to beat. Because they are naturally tender, they're ideal for quick cooking. As well as the familiar chicken breasts, you'll also find goujons (thin strips of breast meat that are superb for stir-fries and curries), escalopes, skinned and flattened chicken breasts and slices of turkey breast. All can be tossed in seasoned flour and pan-fried in less than 5 minutes.

Many of the recipes here are for chicken, but turkey pieces of the same size can be used instead. In this chapter, you'll discover fast versions of favourite dishes such as Easy Chicken Tikka Masala and Chicken Lasagne with Mushroom and Spinach, all of which can be prepared and cooked in the 20-minute time limit.

Lean and healthy, chicken and turkey are full of protein and B vitamins and, if you're trying to reduce your red meat intake, minced (ground) chicken makes an excellent alternative to minced beef, lamb or pork in most dishes.

Chicken and turkey should be eaten within 3–4 days of purchase, so if you're planning to use them in meals later in the week, wrap them well and freeze. They will keep for up to 3 months in the freezer; defrost overnight in the fridge and check that they are completely thawed before cooking. You should also make sure poultry is thoroughly cooked before serving by piercing the flesh at the thickest point; the juices should run clear and not be at all pink.

# Spicy coconut chicken

*Serves 4*
*Ready in* 20 minutes

15 ml/1 tbsp sunflower oil

1 onion, finely sliced

3 skinless, boneless chicken breasts, cut into strips, or a 400 g/14 oz packet of mini chicken fillets

2 tomatoes, roughly chopped

15 ml/1 tbsp red curry paste

400 g/14 oz/large can of coconut milk

15 ml/1 tbsp freshly squeezed or bottled lemon juice

10 ml/2 tsp dark soy sauce

45 ml/3 tbsp fresh or frozen coriander (cilantro)

Salt and freshly ground black pepper

1　Heat the oil in a large non-stick pan, add the onion and cook over a moderately high heat for 2 minutes until beginning to brown.

2　Add the chicken to the pan and cook for 5 minutes until lightly browned and cooked through.

3　Add the tomatoes and curry paste and cook for 1 minute, stirring all the time.

4　Stir in the coconut milk, bring to the boil and simmer for a further 4 minutes.

5　Stir in the lemon juice, soy sauce and most of the coriander. Season with salt and pepper to taste and serve straight away, garnished with the remaining coriander.

*Serve with:* Steamed rice, mangetout (snow peas) and cucumber raita (see below)

## Tips

★　To make a simple cucumber raita, mix together ½ a coarsely grated or finely chopped cucumber, 300 ml/½ pint/1¼ cups of Greek-style yoghurt and 45 ml/3 tbsp of fresh or frozen chopped coriander.

★　To serve four, allow 275 g/10 oz/1¼ cups of long-grain or basmati rice. Thoroughly rinse the rice with cold water, then put in a pan with 600 ml/1 pint/2½ cups of hot vegetable stock, or hot water and a pinch of salt. Bring to the boil, then cover, reduce the heat and simmer for 10–15 minutes or according to the packet instructions until the rice is tender and has absorbed the liquid.

# Chicken and cashew noodle stir-fry

*Serves 4*
*Ready in* 20 minutes

15 ml/1 tbsp clear honey

45 ml/3 tbsp dark soy sauce

10 ml/2 tsp fresh or bottled lemon juice

10 ml/2 tsp fresh or bottled grated root ginger or a large pinch of ground ginger

3 skinless, boneless chicken breasts, diced, or a 400 g/14 oz packet of mini chicken fillets

200 g/7 oz medium egg noodles

5 ml/1 tsp sesame oil

30 ml/2 tbsp sunflower oil

75 g/3 oz/¾ cup cashew nuts

A 350 g/12 oz packet of mixed Chinese stir-fry vegetables

2.5 ml/½ tsp cornflour (cornstarch)

120 ml/4 fl oz/½ cup hot vegetable stock or water

1   Mix together the honey, soy sauce, lemon juice and ginger in a bowl. Add the chicken and toss to coat. Leave to marinate for a few minutes or, if time allows, cover and chill in the fridge for 2 hours.

2   Cook the noodles in boiling lightly salted water for 3–4 minutes or according to the packet instructions until tender. Drain thoroughly, then add the sesame oil, toss and set aside.

3   Meanwhile, heat half the sunflower oil in a wok or large non-stick frying pan. Add the cashew nuts and stir-fry for about 1 minute until golden, then remove from the pan with a slotted spoon, leaving the oil behind. Place the nuts on a plate and set aside.

4   Remove the chicken from the bowl, reserving the marinade, and add to the pan. Stir-fry over a medium-high heat for 5 minutes or until the chicken is cooked through. Remove from the pan with a slotted spoon and add to the cashew nuts.

5   Add the remaining oil to the pan, add the vegetables and stir-fry for 3–4 minutes. Turn the heat down a little, then return the chicken and cashew nuts to the pan.

6   Blend the cornflour with the marinade mixture, then stir in the stock or water. Add this to the pan and bring to the boil, stirring. Add the noodles and stir for a minute or two until piping hot. Serve straight away.

# Easy chicken tikka masala

Serves 4
Ready in 15 minutes

15 ml/1 tbsp sunflower oil

1 onion, finely chopped

5 ml/1 tsp garam masala

A pinch of ground turmeric

A pinch of ground paprika

2 x 200 g/7 oz packets of cooked tikka chicken breast pieces

400 g/14 oz/large can of chopped tomatoes

150 ml/¼ pint/⅔ cup double (heavy) cream

30 ml/2 tbsp chopped fresh or frozen coriander (cilantro)

Salt and freshly ground black pepper

Fresh coriander leaves and sliced red and green chillies to garnish (optional)

1   Heat the oil in a non-stick pan, add the onion and cook over a medium heat for 6–7 minutes until softened and beginning to brown.

2   Stir in the dry spices and cook for a further minute.

3   Add the chicken and tomatoes. Let the mixture bubble for 2–3 minutes, then turn down the heat to low and stir in two-thirds of the cream and the coriander. Heat until steaming hot, stirring occasionally. Season to taste with salt and pepper

4   Remove from the heat and drizzle the rest of the cream over. Scatter with a few coriander leaves and sliced chillies, if liked, before serving.

Serve with: Popadoms and naan bread or basmati rice

## Tips

★   If you prefer, use plain cooked chicken and add 15 ml/1 tbsp of tikka masala or korma paste instead of the dry spices.

★   For a lower-fat version of this dish, use Greek-style yoghurt instead of the double cream (reserve a couple of spoonfuls of the yoghurt for drizzling over the finished dish). Blend 2.5 ml/½ tsp of cornflour (cornstarch) with 5 ml/1 tsp of cold water and stir into the yoghurt before adding to the pan to prevent it from separating.

# Chicken lasagne
## with mushroom and spinach

*Serves 4*
*Ready in* 20 minutes

6 sheets of fresh lasagne
Salt and freshly ground black pepper
15 ml/1 tbsp olive oil
4 skinless, boneless chicken breasts
25 g/1 oz/2 tbsp butter
175 g/6 oz chestnut button mushrooms
100 g/4 oz oyster mushrooms
2 garlic cloves, crushed, or 10 ml/2 tsp garlic purée (paste)
175 g/6 oz young leaf spinach, rinsed
10 ml/2 tsp cornflour (cornstarch)
150 ml/¼ pint/⅔ cup milk
150 ml/¼ pint/⅔ cup single (light) cream
30 ml/2 tbsp ready-grated Parmesan cheese

1   Halve the lasagne widthways with scissors. Place in a bowl, sprinkle with a little salt, then cover with plenty of boiling water. Leave for 10 minutes.

2   Meanwhile, brush a ridged cast iron grill (broiler) pan or a non-stick frying pan with the oil, then place over a moderately high heat. Trim the chicken breasts, if necessary, then slice each in half horizontally. Cook for 3–4 minutes on each side or until lightly browned and cooked through.

3   While the chicken is cooking, melt the butter in a frying pan, add the chestnut mushrooms and cook for 3–4 minutes. Add the oyster mushrooms, garlic and spinach and cook for a further 2 minutes until the spinach has wilted.

4   Blend the cornflour with a little of the milk in a small saucepan, then stir in the rest of the milk and the cream. Bring to the boil, stirring, then simmer for 2 minutes until thickened. Season with salt and pepper.

5   Thoroughly drain the lasagne. On four warmed plates, layer up the lasagne sheets with the chicken, mushroom and spinach mixture and white sauce. Sprinkle with the Parmesan before serving.

# Chicken salad niçoise

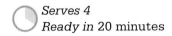
*Serves 4*
*Ready in* 20 minutes

200 g/7 oz fine green beans, trimmed

3 eggs, at room temperature

2 Little Gem lettuces

12 cherry tomatoes, halved

½ cucumber, sliced

1 red onion, thinly sliced

3 cooked chicken breasts, thickly sliced or cubed

75 g/3 oz/½ cup stoned (pitted) black olives

*For the dressing:*

4 anchovy fillets from a jar or can

1 garlic clove, peeled and roughly chopped, or 5 ml/1 tsp garlic purée (paste)

5 ml/1 tsp Dijon mustard

60 ml/4 tbsp olive oil

30 ml/2 tbsp fresh or bottled lemon juice

Freshly ground black pepper

15 ml/1 tbsp chopped fresh or frozen herbs such as parsley, basil and tarragon

1   Put the beans in a pan and pour over enough boiling water to cover. Bring back to the boil and simmer for 3 minutes until tender. Remove from the pan with a slotted spoon and rinse under cold running water to prevent further cooking.

2   Lower the eggs gently into the boiling water using a spoon. Once the water starts to boil again, lower the heat and simmer for 7–8 minutes. Remove the eggs from the water and plunge into cold water (this helps prevent a black ring forming around the yolk). Peel when cool enough to handle and cut each egg into quarters.

3   Place the lettuce leaves in a large bowl, or four individual bowls, with the beans, tomatoes, cucumber and onion slices. Top with the chicken, egg quarters and olives.

4   To make the dressing, put the anchovy fillets and garlic in a small food processor or blender and process for a few seconds. Add the mustard, oil, lemon juice and pepper and blend until smooth and creamy, stopping and scraping down the sides half-way through, if necessary. Stir in the herbs.

5   Drizzle the dressing over the salad or serve separately on the side.

# Chicken and tropical fruit kebabs with couscous

*Serves 4*
*Ready in* 20 minutes

1 firm, ripe mango
Zest and juice of 1 lime
4 skinless, boneless chicken breasts, trimmed and cut into bite-sized pieces
15 ml/1 tbsp fresh or bottled grated root ginger
A small bunch of mint, finely chopped, plus extra to garnish
400 g/14 oz/large can of pineapple chunks in juice, drained
1 lime, cut into 8 wedges
*For the couscous:*
400 ml/14 fl oz/1¾ cups hot vegetable stock
5 ml/1 tsp olive oil
A pinch of ground turmeric
250 g/9 oz/1½ cups couscous

1 Peel and halve the mango, remove the stone (pit) and cut the flesh into bite-sized cubes.

2 Reserve 15 ml/1 tbsp of the lime juice, then place the rest in a non-metallic bowl with the chicken, lime zest, ginger and mint. Mix together, then leave for a few minutes for the flavours to mingle.

3 Meanwhile, begin cooking the couscous. Pour the stock into a saucepan and add the oil and turmeric. Bring to the boil, then pour in the couscous in a steady stream and stir thoroughly. Turn off the heat, cover with a lid and leave to stand for 5 minutes.

4 Preheat the grill (broiler) to moderately hot and line the grill pan with foil. Thread the chicken pieces, pineapple chunks, mango cubes and wedges of lime on to eight pre-soaked wooden skewers. Place on the grill rack and cook for 3–4 minutes on each side or until browned and cooked through.

5 Sprinkle the reserved lime juice over the couscous, then heat gently for 1 minute, stirring with a fork to separate the grains. Divide the couscous between four warmed plates, top with the kebabs and garnish with mint.

## Tip

★ Peel 2.5 cm/1 in pieces of fresh root ginger, wrap in freezer film and freeze. It's much easier to grate when frozen and you'll always have a ready supply.

# Creamy turkey stroganoff
## with mushrooms

*Serves 4*
*Ready in* 20 minutes

30 ml/2 tbsp olive oil

350 g/12 oz turkey breast steaks, cut into strips

1 red onion, sliced

250 g/9 oz large chestnut mushrooms, quartered

1 garlic clove, chopped, or 5 ml/1 tsp garlic purée (paste)

5 ml/1 tsp ground paprika

150 ml/¼ pint/⅔ cup chicken stock

75 ml/5 tbsp crème fraîche

15 ml/1 tbsp chopped fresh or frozen parsley

Salt and freshly ground black pepper

1   Heat half the oil in a large non-stick frying pan or wok. Add the turkey and fry over a high heat for 2–3 minutes or until golden. Lift out with a slotted spoon and transfer to a plate, leaving the juices behind in the pan.

2   Add the remaining oil to the pan, add the onion and cook, stirring, for 3 minutes.

3   Add the mushrooms, garlic and paprika to the pan and cook for 2 minutes, stirring frequently.

4   Stir in the stock and return the turkey and any juices to the pan. Bring the mixture to a simmer and cook gently, uncovered, for 5 minutes.

5   Stir in the crème fraîche and parsley and season to taste with salt and pepper. Let the mixture bubble for 1 minute before serving.

*Serve with:* Brown or white rice, runner beans and griddled courgettes (zucchini)

## Tips

★   You could also make this dish with the same weight of turkey escalopes or chicken breasts.

★   Chestnut mushrooms are darker in colour and more strongly flavoured than ordinary button mushrooms, but either could be used for this dish.

# Italian turkey escalopes

*Serves 4*
*Ready in* 20 minutes

4 x 125 g/4½ oz turkey breast steaks

4 slices of Parma ham

12 large fresh basil leaves

30 ml/2 tbsp plain (all-purpose) flour

Salt and freshly ground black pepper

30 ml/2 tbsp olive oil

150 ml/¼ pint/⅔ cup dry Marsala or Madeira

60 ml/4 tbsp chicken or vegetable stock

1  Place the turkey breast steaks between two pieces of oiled clingfilm (plastic wrap) or baking parchment and use a rolling pin to gently bat the meat out thinly.

2  Remove the clingfilm or parchment and lay a slice of ham on top of each escalope. Using wooden cocktail sticks (toothpicks), pin three basil leaves to each escalope, securing the turkey, ham and basil together.

3  Lightly season the flour with salt and pepper, then dip the escalopes in the flour to coat.

4  Heat the oil in a large non-stick frying pan over a moderate heat. Add the turkey escalopes to the pan, ham side down, and cook for 2 minutes on each side or until the turkey is cooked through. Transfer to warmed serving plates.

5  Add the Marsala or Madeira and stock to the pan and bubble over a high heat for about 3 minutes or until reduced and syrupy. Drizzle the sauce over the turkey escalopes and serve straight away.

*Serve with:* Griddled courgettes (zucchini) and sautéed potatoes

## Tip

★  For sautéed potatoes, allow 175–225 g (6–8 oz) of boiled potatoes per person. Cut the potatoes into 2 cm/¾ in cubes and fry in a mixture of hot melted unsalted (sweet) butter and sunflower or olive oil, turning frequently, until crisp and golden on all sides. If liked, flavour with some roughly chopped rosemary leaves. Sprinkle with a little salt and pepper before serving.

# Turkey frittata
## with mixed vegetables

*Serves 4*
*Ready in* 20 minutes

15 ml/1 tbsp olive oil
1 onion, finely sliced
1 garlic clove, crushed, or 5 ml/1 tsp garlic purée (paste)
350 g/12 oz skinless and boneless ready-cooked turkey, cubed
175 g/6 oz frozen mixed vegetables
6 eggs
30 ml/2 tbsp chopped fresh or frozen parsley
5 ml/1 tsp ground paprika
Salt and freshly ground black pepper

1   Heat the oil in a heavy-based non-stick frying pan about 25 cm/10 in in diameter. Add the onion and cook over a medium heat for 7–8 minutes until softened and just starting to brown.

2   Add the garlic, turkey and vegetables and cook for a further 2–3 minutes.

3   Meanwhile, whisk the eggs with the parsley, paprika and salt and pepper. Pour the egg mixture over the turkey and vegetables in the frying pan and cook for 3–4 minutes or until the egg has set on the base, lifting the edges to allow the uncooked egg mixture to run on to the pan.

4   Preheat the grill (broiler) to high. When there is just a little uncooked egg on the top, place the pan under the grill and cook for a further 2 minutes to set and brown the top.

5   Loosen the edges of the frittata then slide it on to a plate or board and allow to firm and cool for a minute. Cut into wedges and serve warm or leave to cool completely before cutting and serving.

*Serve with:* A cucumber and tomato salad

## Tip

★   Instead of mixed vegetables, use the same weight of cold leftover potatoes or vegetables such as green beans, peas or courgettes (zucchini). Fresh tarragon or chives may be used instead of the parsley. For a spicy frittata, add 2.5 ml/½ tsp of dried chilli flakes to the beaten egg mixture.

# beef, pork & lamb

Meat is wonderfully flavoursome and lends itself well to all sorts of flavours and seasonings for every taste and budget. In this chapter you'll find a wide range of meat dishes from beef steaks and lamb noisettes to minced (ground) meats, all ideal for meals in minutes. Here, you can sample tastes from all around the world, from Thai-style Pork and Cantonese Sweet and Sour Beef to Lamb and Vegetable Pilaff.

Beef, lamb and pork provide an excellent concentrated source of protein and many valuable nutrients, particularly the minerals iron and zinc. They can be healthily lean too, with some cuts containing no more fat than chicken. Quick-cooking cuts of meat – perfect for stir-frying, grilling (broiling) and pan-frying – tend to be the tender prime cuts such as steak and tenderloin; but, although they are more expensive, there's no wastage and a little can go a long way.

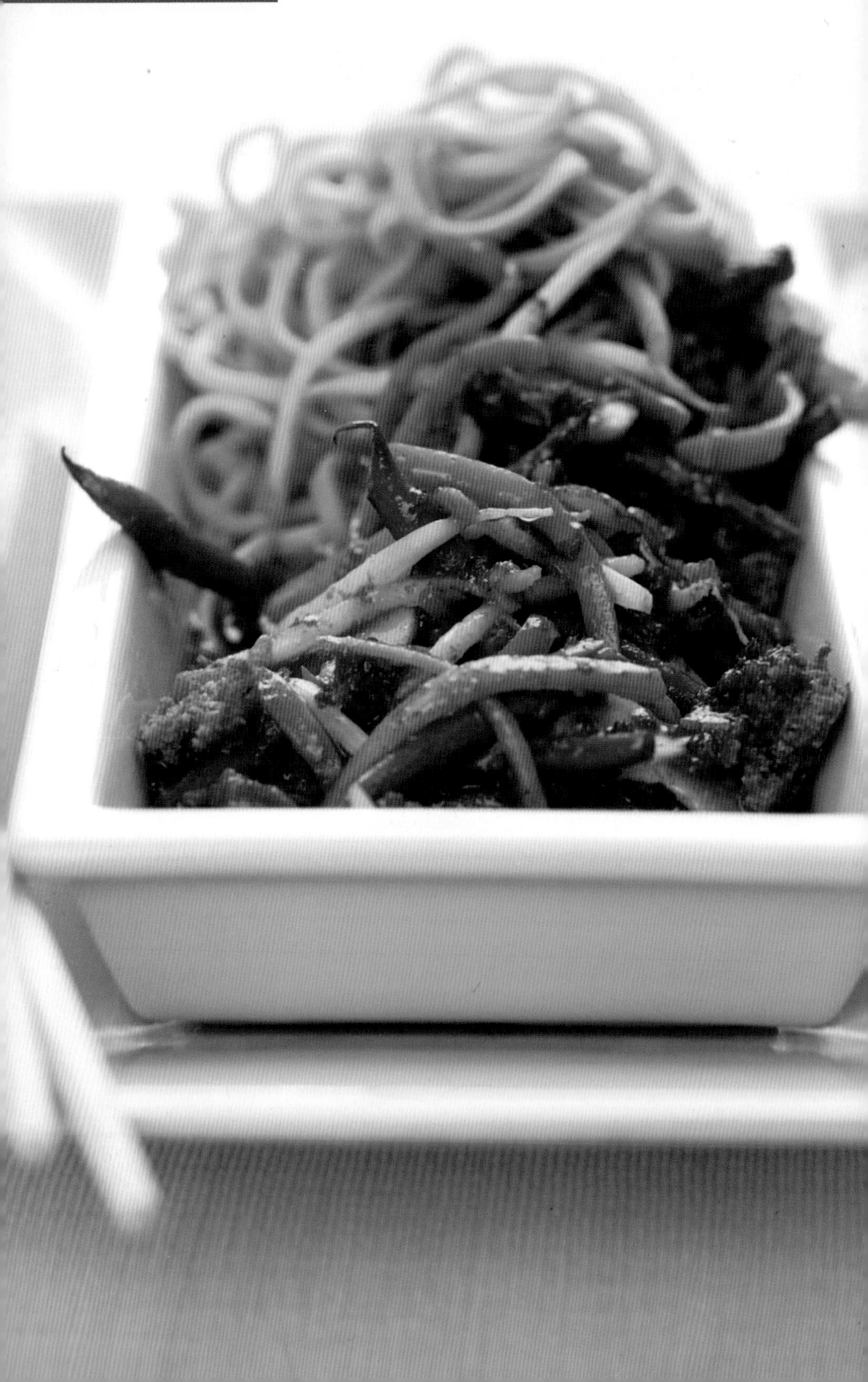

# Chilli corned beef
## with noodles

*Serves 4*
*Ready in* 20 minutes

30 ml/2 tbsp sunflower oil

2 garlic cloves, crushed

5 ml/1 tsp fresh or bottled grated root ginger

200 g/7 oz mushrooms, thinly sliced

200 g/7 oz green beans, halved

1 carrot, peeled and cut into matchsticks

6 spring onions (scallions), thinly sliced

50 g/2 oz/1 cup beansprouts

350 g/12 oz/medium can of corned beef, cut into bite-size cubes

15 ml/1 tbsp dark soy sauce

15 ml/1 tbsp hoisin sauce

30 ml/2 tbsp sweet chilli sauce

30 ml/2 tbsp cold water

250 g/9 oz medium egg noodles

**1** Heat the oil in a large non-stick frying pan or wok, add the garlic and ginger and cook for 30 seconds, stirring all the time. Add the mushrooms, beans and carrot and stir-fry for 3–4 minutes.

**2** Add the spring onions and beansprouts and stir-fry for a further 1–2 minutes, then stir in the corned beef.

**3** Mix the soy, hoisin and chilli sauces with the water and add to the pan. Stir to coat the ingredients evenly and let the mixture bubble for a minute.

**4** Meanwhile, cook the noodles in boiling water for 3–4 minutes or according to the packet instructions until tender. Drain thoroughly, then divide between four warmed bowls or plates. Spoon the beef and vegetable mixture over the noodles and serve straight away.

## Tip

★ For an even quicker stir-fry, use a 500 g/18 oz packet of stir-fry vegetables instead of the mushrooms, beans, carrot, spring onions and beansprouts.

# **Fruity beef salad** with
## mustard and ginger dressing

*Serves 4*
*Ready in* 20 minutes

2 thick-cut lean sirloin steaks, about 400 g/14 oz in total, trimmed of fat

Salt and freshly ground black pepper

150 g/5 oz/2½ cups beansprouts, rinsed

A 100 g/4 oz bag of herb or baby salad leaves

100 g/4 oz red grapes, halved

*For the dressing:*

10 ml/2 tsp fresh or bottled grated root ginger

10 ml/2 tsp Dijon or wholegrain mustard

10 ml/2 tsp white wine vinegar

30 ml/2 tbsp sunflower oil

15 ml/1 tbsp hazelnut (filbert) or walnut oil

**1** Rub the steaks with half the sunflower oil from the dressing, then lightly season with salt and pepper. Heat a ridged cast iron grill (broiler) pan or a non-stick frying pan, add the steaks and grill (broil) over a high heat for 2–5 minutes. Turn them over and cook for a further 2–5 minutes. Remove the steaks to a board and leave to rest for a few minutes (this helps tenderise the meat), then carve into thin slices.

**2** Meanwhile, to make the dressing, put the ginger, mustard, vinegar, remaining sunflower oil and the hazelnut or walnut oil in a screw-topped jar. Shake well to mix the ingredients together.

**3** Mix together the beansprouts, salad leaves, grapes and two-thirds of the dressing. Arrange in a shallow salad bowl or on individual plates and top with the beef. Drizzle with the remaining dressing and serve straight away.

*Serve with:* Warm crusty French bread

## Tips

★ If preferred, use 60 ml/4 tbsp of bought dressing, such as mango and red (bell) pepper dressing.

★ Four 100 g/4 oz beef medallion steaks may be used instead of the sirloin steak.

★ A 2 cm/¾ in thick steak will take about 2 minutes on each side for rare, 3–4 minutes for medium and 5–6 minutes for well done.

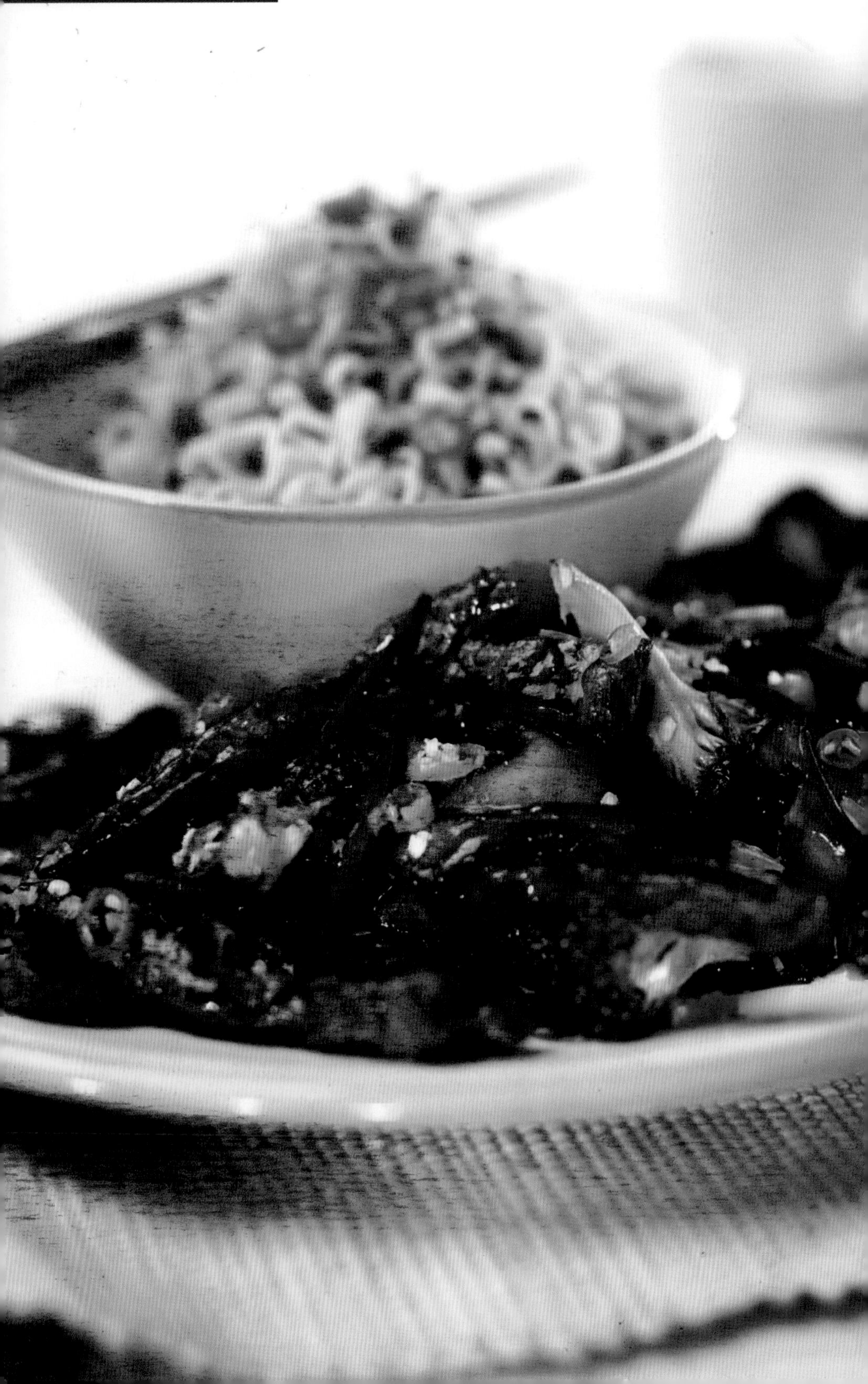

# Beef and mushroom sauté

*Serves 4*
*Ready in* 20 minutes

400 g/14 oz lean rump steak

5 ml/1 tsp sesame oil

250 g/9 oz medium egg noodles

30 ml/2 tbsp sunflower oil

1 garlic clove, thinly sliced, or 5 ml/1 tsp garlic purée (paste)

100 g/4 oz shiitake or chestnut mushrooms, thinly sliced

200 g/7 oz small broccoli florets

75 ml/5 tbsp oyster sauce

Sliced red and green chillies to garnish (optional)

**1** Trim any fat from the steak, then cut the meat across the grain into thin slices. Put in a bowl and drizzle the sesame oil over. Toss the meat to lightly coat in the oil. Set aside.

**2** Cook the noodles in a saucepan of boiling lightly salted water for 4 minutes, or cook or soak them according to the packet instructions. Drain the noodles in a colander and cover with the pan lid to keep them warm.

**3** While the noodles are cooking, heat a wok or heavy-based non-stick frying pan until hot, add half the sunflower oil and swirl to coat the wok. Add the beef and garlic and stir-fry for 2 minutes or until the beef is browned all over. Remove from the pan with a slotted spoon and set aside.

**4** Heat the remaining sunflower oil in the pan until hot, then add the mushrooms and broccoli. Stir-fry for 2 minutes or until the mushrooms begin to colour. Return the beef and its juices to the pan, then add the oyster sauce and simmer for 1 minute.

**5** Transfer to a warmed serving dish or individual plates and scatter with chilli slices, if liked. Serve with the noodles.

## Tips

★ Thinly sliced boneless lean pork loin may be used instead of the beef, if preferred. Instead of oyster sauce, use 60 ml/4 tbsp of bottled yellow bean sauce blended with 15 ml/1 tbsp of vegetable stock or water and 15 ml/1 tbsp of light soy sauce.

★ Other vegetables could be included in this dish, such as thinly sliced carrots, sliced spring onions (scallions) or sliced red or yellow (bell) peppers. Add them to the pan with the mushrooms and broccoli.

# Cantonese sweet and sour beef

*Serves 4*
*Ready in* 20 minutes

10 ml/2 tsp cornflour (cornstarch)

5 ml/1 tsp caster (superfine) sugar

30 ml/2 tbsp dark soy sauce

60 ml/4 tbsp juice from a can of pineapple rings

15 ml/1 tbsp dry sherry

10 ml/2 tsp white or red wine vinegar

2 lean rump steaks, about 400 g/14 oz in total

10 ml/2 tsp sunflower oil

1 garlic clove, crushed, or 5 ml/1 tsp garlic purée (paste)

5 ml/1 tsp fresh or bottled grated root ginger

4 spring onions (scallions) sliced

1 green (bell) pepper, seeded and diced

4 canned pineapple rings, chopped

**1** Blend the cornflour and sugar with the soy sauce, then stir in the pineapple juice, sherry and vinegar. Set aside.

**2** Trim any visible fat from the steaks and cut the meat into thin strips about 1 cm/½ in wide. Mix the strips with the oil until they are lightly coated. Heat a large non-stick frying pan or wok over a moderately high heat, add the steak and stir-fry for 2 minutes until browned.

**3** Add the garlic, ginger, spring onions and diced pepper and stir-fry for a further 2 minutes. Add the pineapple, then pour in the sauce and stir until it bubbles and thickens. Simmer for 1 minute before serving.

*Serve with:* Steamed or boiled rice

## Tips

★ Stir-frying is one of the fastest and easiest methods of cooking. Prepare all the ingredients before you start to cook; once stir-frying starts, there's no time for chopping and slicing.

★ Spring onions (scallions) are a great buy when you're cooking in a hurry. Keep them in a paper or open plastic bag (to allow air to circulate) in the salad drawer of the fridge.

# Spiced minced beef
## and pea curry

*Serves 4*
*Ready in* 20 minutes

15 ml/1 tbsp sunflower oil
400 g/14 oz lean minced (ground) beef
1 onion, very finely chopped
30 ml/2 tbsp medium curry paste
100 g/4 oz potatoes, peeled and cut into 1 cm/½ in dice
200 g/7 oz thawed frozen peas
200 g/7 oz cherry tomatoes, halved
60 ml/4 tbsp beef or vegetable stock
Salt
15 ml/1 tbsp freshly squeezed or bottled lemon juice
Fresh mint leaves to garnish (optional)

**1** Heat the oil in a large non-stick frying pan or wok. Add the beef and cook over a high heat, stirring with a wooden spoon to break up the meat, for about 5 minutes until lightly browned.

**2** Push the meat to one side of the pan and add the onion. Reduce the heat a little and cook for 5-6 minutes, stirring occasionally, until the onion is softened and lightly browned.

**3** Stir in the curry paste and cook for 1 minute, then stir in the potatoes, peas, tomatoes and stock. Cover the pan and cook for 5 minutes over a medium heat, stirring occasionally, until the potatoes are tender.

**4** Remove from the heat, season to taste with salt and stir in the lemon juice. Garnish with mint leaves, if liked, and serve straight away.

*Serve with:* Warmed naan bread, popadoms and thick plain yoghurt

## Tip

★ This traditional mellow curry is called *keema* in India and may be made with lean minced lamb instead of beef. For a fruity version, add 50 g/ 2 oz/⅓ cup of sultanas (golden raisins) and 1 peeled and chopped eating (dessert) apple with the potato. If preferred, a 200 g/7 oz/small can of chopped tomatoes can be used instead of the cherry tomatoes.

# Thai-style pork

*Serves 4*
*Ready in* 20 minutes

5 ml/1 tsp sunflower oil

450 g/1 lb lean minced (ground) pork

1 red (bell) pepper, seeded and diced

150 g/5 oz mushrooms, sliced

15 ml/1 tbsp cornflour (cornstarch)

30 ml/2 tbsp light soy sauce

Juice of 1 lime

150 ml/¼ pint/⅔ cup vegetable or beef stock

Salt and freshly ground black pepper

30 ml/2 tbsp chopped fresh or frozen coriander (cilantro)

**1** Heat the oil in a large non-stick frying pan or wok. Add the pork and cook over a high heat, stirring with a wooden spoon to break up the meat, for about 5 minutes until lightly browned.

**2** Add the diced pepper and mushrooms to the pan and cook for 2–3 minutes, stirring the mixture frequently.

**3** Blend the cornflour with the soy sauce and lime juice in a jug. Stir in the stock. Pour into the pan and bring to the boil, stirring all the time until thickened. Simmer for 5 minutes.

**4** Taste the mixture and season with salt and pepper. Stir in the coriander and serve straight away.

*Serve with:* Steamed or boiled rice

## Tip

★ This dish can be made in advance, cooled and kept covered in the fridge for up to 24 hours. You may also consider making double the quantity and freezing half for a later date.

# Spicy pork and apricot curry

*Serves 4*
*Ready in* 20 minutes

15 ml/1 tbsp sunflower oil
400 g/14 oz pork tenderloin or fillet, cut into thin slices or strips
1 small onion, finely chopped
5 ml/1 tsp fresh or bottled grated root ginger
2 garlic cloves, crushed, or 10 ml/2 tsp garlic purée (paste)
1 red chilli, halved, seeded and thinly sliced, or 2.5 ml/½ tsp dried chilli flakes
5 ml/1 tsp cumin seeds
250 ml/8 fl oz/1 cup passata (sieved tomatoes)
150 ml/¼ pint/⅔ cup vegetable stock
175 g/6 oz/1 cup ready-to-eat dried apricots
Salt and freshly ground black pepper
45 ml/3 tbsp chopped fresh or frozen coriander (cilantro)
Sprigs of coriander to garnish (optional)

**1** Heat the oil in a large non-stick frying pan or wok. When hot, add the pork and stir-fry over a high heat until the meat is lightly browned. Add the onion and continue to stir-fry for 2–3 minutes.

**2** Stir in the ginger, garlic, chilli and cumin. Cook for a few seconds, add the passata and stock and bring to the boil. Add the apricots and reduce the heat to medium. Cook for 5–6 minutes until the meat is cooked through and tender.

**3** Remove the curry from the heat and season to taste. Stir in the chopped coriander and garnish with sprigs of coriander, if liked, before serving.

*Serve with:* Pilau rice, steamed greens and mini popadoms

## Tips

★ Take care when preparing fresh chillies and always wash your hands thoroughly afterwards as the juices can cause burning irritation, especially if you touch your eyes or lips.

★ If you enjoy spicy food, it's worth investing in a small jar of ready-chopped chillies, which will save on preparation time. About 5 ml/1 tsp is the equivalent of 1 small fresh red chilli. Once opened, it will keep in the fridge for 2–3 months.

# Hoisin pork skewers

*Serves 4*
*Ready in* 20 minutes

450 g/1 lb lean pork
60 ml/4 tbsp hoisin sauce
1 large red (bell) pepper, halved, seeded and cut into strips
100 g/4 oz mangetout (snow peas)
150 g/5 oz thin stir-fry rice noodles

**1** Trim the pork of any excess fat, then cut into bite-sized pieces. Put the meat in a bowl with the hoisin sauce and stir to ensure it is thoroughly coated. Leave to marinate for a few minutes while preparing the vegetables or, if you are preparing in advance, for up to 4 hours in the fridge (this will help to tenderise and flavour the meat).

**2** Meanwhile, if you are using wooden skewers, soak four in cold water; this helps stop them charring when grilling (broiling).

**3** Preheat the grill to medium and line the grill pan with foil. Thread the meat on to the soaked wooden or metal skewers, alternating with the pepper strips and mangetout and place on the grill rack. Cook for 12–15 minutes, turning occasionally, until the pork is browned and cooked through.

**4** Meanwhile, place the noodles in a heatproof bowl and cover with boiling water. Set aside for 5 minutes or until tender, then drain thoroughly and serve with the pork skewers.

## Tips

★ Hoisin sauce is a thick and sticky brownish-red sauce usually made from soy beans, garlic, chilli, sugar and vinegar. You'll find it among the oriental cooking sauces at the supermarket. Once opened, it will keep in the fridge for several months.

★ This dish is also good made with thickly cut lamb steaks or shoulder of lamb, cut into cubes.

# Rosemary lamb and potato kebabs with soured cream

*Serves 4*
*Ready in* 20 minutes

12 baby new potatoes, cut in half
Salt and freshly ground black pepper
450 g/1 lb lamb neck fillet
45 ml/3 tbsp olive oil
5 ml/1 tsp red wine vinegar
2 small courgettes (zucchini), diagonally sliced
30 ml/2 tbsp chopped fresh rosemary
150 ml/¼ pint/⅔ cup soured (dairy sour) cream
30 ml/2 tbsp chopped fresh mint

**1** Put the potatoes in a small saucepan and pour over just enough boiling water to cover. Add a large pinch of salt, then bring to the boil. Turn down the heat a little, half-cover the pan with a lid and simmer for 5 minutes or until just tender. Drain and set aside.

**2** Meanwhile, trim the lamb of any excess fat, then cut into bite-sized pieces. Whisk together 15 ml/1 tbsp of the oil and the vinegar in a bowl, add the lamb and toss to lightly coat.

**3** Thread the lamb, potatoes and courgettes on to eight metal or soaked wooden skewers. Mix together the remaining oil with the rosemary and brush over the kebabs.

**4** Heat a ridged cast iron grill (broiler) pan or heavy non-stick frying pan until hot. Place the kebabs on the pan and cook for 8–10 minutes, turning occasionally, until the courgettes are tender and the lamb is cooked to your liking. (If preferred, cook the kebabs on a grill pan under a moderately hot pre-heated grill.)

**5** Mix together the soured cream and mint and season with salt and pepper. Spoon into a small bowl and serve as a dip with the kebabs.

*Serve with:* Warmed pitta breads

## Tip

★ If preparing ahead, toss the lamb in the oil and vinegar mixture and leave to marinate in the fridge for several hours (this will help to tenderise and flavour the meat).

# Lamb noisettes
## with almond and lemon

*Serves 4*
*Ready in* 20 minutes

½ lemon
30 ml/2 tbsp olive oil
100 g/4 oz flaked (slivered) almonds
A pinch of freshly grated nutmeg
8 small lamb noisettes, about 75 g/3 oz each
25 g/1 oz/2 tbsp butter
Salt and freshly ground black pepper
Sprigs of rosemary to garnish (optional)

**1** Halve the lemon and roughly chop up one quarter. Squeeze the juice from the other half.

**2** Place the chopped lemon, half the oil, half the almonds and the nutmeg in a food processor and whiz to form a smooth paste. Spread this mixture on the noisettes.

**3** Heat the remaining oil in a large non-stick frying pan, add the noisettes and cook over a medium heat for 3–5 minutes on each side, depending on how well done you wish the lamb to be.

**4** When the noisettes are almost done to your liking, add the butter with the remaining almonds and sauté gently for 1–2 minutes until lightly browned. Watch the nuts carefully as they burn easily.

**5** Transfer the cooked noisettes to warmed plates. Add the lemon juice to the pan and stir into the juices. Lightly season with salt and pepper, then pour the pan juices over the noisettes and serve straight away garnished with sprigs of rosemary, if liked.

*Serve with:* Boiled baby new potatoes and vegetables such as peas, courgettes (zucchini) or green beans

## Tip

★ Noisettes are cut from the loin or best end of lamb and most butchers will prepare them for you on request. Lamb cutlets make a good and cheaper alternative.

# Lamb and vegetable pilaff

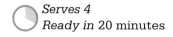
*Serves 4*
*Ready in* 20 minutes

350 g/12 oz/1½ cups easy-cook basmati or long-grain rice, rinsed

400 g/14 oz lean minced (ground) lamb

250 g/9 oz frozen mixed vegetables

30 ml/2 tbsp medium curry paste

150 ml/¼ pint/⅔ cup vegetable stock

Salt and freshly ground black pepper

4 hard-boiled (hard-cooked) eggs, peeled and halved

**1** Cook the rice in a large pan of boiling water for 10–12 minutes or according to the packet instructions until tender. Drain thoroughly.

**2** While the rice is cooking, heat a large non-stick frying pan over a high heat. Add the lamb and stir-fry for 3–4 minutes or until lightly browned.

**3** Add the vegetables, curry paste and stock and cook, stirring, over a high heat for 5–6 minutes or until the vegetables are tender and only a little of the stock remains.

**4** Add the cooked rice and cook, stirring all the time, for 1–2 minutes or until everything is steaming hot. Taste and season with salt and pepper.

**5** Divide the rice mixture between four warmed serving plates and top with the eggs. Serve straight away.

## Tip

★ To cook hard-boiled eggs, use eggs at room temperature (if used straight from the fridge they may crack) and lower them gently into a pan of boiling water using a spoon. Once the water starts to boil again, lower the heat and simmer for 7–8 minutes. Remove the eggs from the water and plunge into cold water (this helps prevent a black ring forming around the yolk). Leave until cool before cracking the shell and peeling.

# fish & seafood

Delicious, healthy and versatile, the best way to cook fish is fast, making it ideal for super-quick suppers. It's also a very healthy choice as it's a great source of protein and provides many vitamins and minerals.

You should eat oily fish such as salmon, tuna or mackerel at least once a week as it contains beneficial heart-healthy fats. Try Warm Salmon and Bean Salad with Parmesan Croûtons or Lemon Peppered Mackerel with Sweet Potato Mash and Curly Kale. White fish has very lean flesh and is low in fat. For speed, make the most of fresh and frozen fish portions and bags of ready-prepared seafood. Try using canned and smoked fish as well as fresh, which needs little preparation.

When buying fish, remember that if it's really fresh it shouldn't smell 'fishy'. Obviously, it's difficult to test pre-packed fish for freshness, but make sure that it looks firm and moist and buy from a reliable source. Both fresh and frozen seafood should be put in the fridge or freezer as soon as possible and, ideally, fresh fish should be eaten on the day you buy it.

# Fish fingers and bean
## pitta pockets

*Serves 4*
*Ready in* 20 minutes

8 frozen fish fingers
Finely grated zest and juice of 1 lemon
75 ml/5 tbsp mayonnaise
15 ml/1 tbsp sweet chilli sauce
200 g/7 oz/small can of borlotti or cannellini beans, drained and rinsed
2 Little Gem lettuces, finely shredded
4 large pitta breads
30 ml/2 tbsp fresh or frozen chopped parsley
*For the salad:*
2 large oranges, segmented
1 red onion, halved and thinly sliced
12 stoned (pitted) black olives
Salt and freshly ground black pepper
Diced red (bell) pepper to garnish (optional)

1   Cook the fish fingers according to the packet instructions, cut into bite-sized pieces and set aside.

2   Put the lemon zest, 15 ml/1 tbsp of the lemon juice, the mayonnaise and chilli sauce in a bowl and stir together. Stir in the beans, followed by the lettuce and fish finger pieces.

3   Heat a ridged cast iron grill (broiler) pan over a high heat and grill (broil) the pitta breads for about a minute on each side, then cut them in half. Gently open them up to make pockets and spoon in the fish finger mixture.

4   To make the salad, combine the orange segments and their juice with the onion and olives. Lightly season with salt and pepper.

5   Place two filled pitta halves on each of four plates, garnish with diced pepper, if liked, and arrange the salad on the side. Serve straight away.

## Tip

★   For a vegetarian version of this dish, substitute eight vegetarian sausages for the fish fingers. Grill or fry according to the packet instructions, then cut into bite-sized pieces.

# Seafood skewers

*Serves 4*
*Ready in* 20 minutes

24 raw tiger prawns (shrimp), peeled

400 g/14 oz skinless cod loin or monkfish, cut into large cubes

Finely grated zest and juice of 1 lemon

A small bunch of basil leaves, roughly torn, plus extra for garnish

Salt and freshly ground black pepper

2 avocados, peeled and roughly chopped

30 ml/2 tbsp olive oil

1 If you are using wooden skewers, soak eight in cold water for a few minutes; this helps stop them charring when grilling (broiling).

2 Put the prawns, fish, most of the lemon zest (reserve some for garnish), the lemon juice and basil in a shallow non-metallic bowl. Season with salt and pepper and stir thoroughly.

3 Preheat the grill (broiler) to high and line the grill pan with foil. Thread the prawns and fish on to eight skewers. Place on the grill rack and cook for 3 minutes on each side or until cooked through.

4 Pile the chopped avocado on the centre of each serving plate and scatter the reserved lemon zest over. Arrange the skewers around the avocado. Drizzle with the oil and garnish with basil leaves.

*Serve with:* A mixed leaf and tomato salad

## Tips

★ Any firm thick white fish can be used for these skewers, including unsmoked haddock and coley. Ask for advice at the fish counter when buying.

★ Use a flavoured oil instead of the olive oil for extra flavour, if liked. Both chilli oil and basil-flavoured oil would work well here.

# Spicy seafood pasta
## with chilli

*Serves 4*
*Ready in* 15 minutes

400 g/14 oz dried quick-cook penne

15 ml/1 tbsp olive oil

1 garlic clove, crushed, or 5 ml/1 tsp garlic purée (paste)

2 shallots, peeled and finely chopped

A 400 g/14 oz bag of mixed cooked seafood, thawed if frozen

400 g/14 oz/large can of chopped tomatoes with chilli

1 hot red chilli, halved, seeded and finely chopped, or 2.5 ml/½ tsp dried chilli flakes

15 ml/1 tbsp snipped fresh chives or chopped fresh or frozen parsley

Salt and freshly ground black pepper

**1** Cook the pasta in a large pan of boiling salted water for 3–4 minutes or according to the packet instructions until *al dente* (tender, but still with a little 'bite').

**2** Meanwhile, heat the oil in a large non-stick frying pan, add the garlic and shallots and fry for 2–3 minutes until the shallots have softened. Stir in the seafood, tomatoes and chilli, season with salt and pepper and simmer for 2–3 minutes.

**3** Drain the pasta in a colander. Return it to the pan, then add the seafood sauce and gently mix together.

**4** Divide the pasta between four warmed serving bowls and serve straight away, garnished with snipped chives or a sprinkling of parsley.

*Serve with:* Slices of warm olive or rosemary focaccia

## Tips

★ You'll find mixed seafood at the fish counter or in the frozen fish section. The contents may vary, but will usually be a combination of prawns (shrimp), mussels and squid.

★ You could make this pasta dish with strips of shredded cooked chicken instead of seafood.

★ For extra flavour, cook the pasta in vegetable stock instead of water.

# Oriental fish parcels

*Serves 4*
*Ready in* 20 minutes

15 g/½ oz/1 tbsp softened butter or 15 ml/1 tbsp olive oil

4 white fish portions such as cod or haddock, fresh or frozen

10 ml/2 tsp fresh or bottled grated root ginger

1 red chilli, seeded and thinly sliced, or 2.5 ml/½ tsp dried chilli flakes

60 ml/4 tbsp dark soy sauce

10 ml/2 tsp sesame oil

A 300 g/11 oz packet of stir-fry vegetables

1  Preheat the oven to 200°C/400°F/gas 6/fan oven 180°C. Cut out four 30 cm/12 in squares of foil or baking parchment. Grease the squares with the butter or oil to about 5 cm/2 in from the edges.

2  Put a fish portion in the middle of each square. Mix together the ginger, chilli, soy sauce and sesame oil and drizzle half over the fish. Divide the stir-fry vegetables between the squares, then drizzle with the remaining ginger mixture.

3  Fold the top and bottom of each foil or parchment square over the fish and vegetables. Pull the sides together and seal to make a parcel. Put the parcels on a baking tray, then bake in the oven for 14 minutes for fresh fish, 16–18 minutes for frozen fish.

4  Open the parcels carefully as the steam inside will be very hot. Transfer the fillets with a fish slice to warmed plates, then spoon the vegetables and juices over them.

*Serve with:* Rice (cellophane) noodles or egg noodles

## Tip

★  If using rice noodles, put them in a bowl and pour boiling water over. Soak for 3–4 minutes, then drain thoroughly. If using egg noodles, cook them in a pan of lightly salted boiling water or vegetable stock for extra flavour for 3–4 minutes or according to the packet instructions. Drain thoroughly and serve.

# Speedy prawn stir-fry

*Serves* 4
*Ready in* 15 minutes

400 g/14 oz peeled raw tiger prawns (shrimp)

5 ml/1 tsp Chinese five-spice powder

30 ml/2 tbsp sunflower oil

1 garlic clove, thinly sliced, or 5 ml/1 tsp garlic purée (paste)

10 ml/2 tsp fresh or bottled grated root ginger

6 spring onions (scallions), sliced

1 red (bell) pepper, halved, seeded and sliced

1 yellow pepper, halved, seeded and sliced

200 g/7 oz sugar snap peas, halved

200 g/7 oz baby sweetcorn, halved lengthways

100 g/4 oz/2 cups beansprouts

30 ml/2 tbsp clear honey

30 ml/2 tbsp freshly squeezed or bottled lemon juice

30 ml/2 tbsp dark soy sauce

30 ml/2 tbsp cold water

1 Toss the prawns in the five-spice powder to coat. Heat half the oil in a large non-stick frying pan or wok over a high heat. When hot, add the prawns and stir-fry for 2–3 minutes or until pink all over. Remove from the pan and set aside.

2 Heat the remaining oil in the pan. Add the garlic, ginger, spring onions, sliced peppers, sugar snap peas and sweetcorn. Stir-fry for 2 minutes, then add the beansprouts and cook for a further 2–3 minutes or until the vegetables are almost tender.

3 Mix together the honey, lemon juice, soy sauce and water. Add to the pan and cook for just a few seconds. Return the prawns to the pan and cook for 1–2 minutes or until everything is hot.

4 Divide between four warmed bowls and serve straight away.

*Serve with:* Sticky jasmine rice or noodles

## Tip

★ Chinese five-spice powder adds lots of flavour to this simple stir-fry. It contains finely ground cinnamon, star anise, ginger and fennel seeds.

# Prawn and vegetable biryani

**Serves** 4
**Ready in** 20 minutes

15 ml/1 tbsp sunflower oil
2 courgettes (zucchini), trimmed and diced
1 red (bell) pepper, halved, seeded and diced
5 ml/1 tsp ground coriander
5 ml/1 tsp ground cumin
300 g/10 oz/1¼ cups basmati rice, rinsed
600 ml/1 pint/2½ cups hot vegetable stock
Salt and freshly ground black pepper
250 g/9 oz cooked tiger prawns (shrimp), thawed if frozen
30 ml/2 tbsp fresh or frozen chopped coriander (cilantro)
Fresh coriander leaves and wedges of lime to garnish (optional)

1 Heat the oil in a large saucepan, preferably non-stick, add the courgettes and red pepper and stir-fry for 1 minute. Add the dry spices and cook for a further minute, stirring all the time, then stir in the rice.

2 Pour in the stock and season with salt and pepper to taste. Bring to the boil, reduce the heat, cover with a lid and simmer for 10 minutes.

3 Stir in the prawns and coriander, re-cover the pan and simmer for a further minute or until the prawns are hot, the vegetables are cooked and the rice is tender and has absorbed the liquid.

4 Leave the biryani to stand for a minute, then spoon into warmed bowls and serve straight away garnished with sprigs of fresh coriander and wedges of lime, if liked.

*Serve with:* Cucumber raita (see page 45) or a bowl of thick plain yoghurt and warm naan breads

## Tip

★ For a fruity biryani, add 50 g/2 oz/⅓ cup of sultanas (golden raisins) or chopped dried apricots with the prawns and chopped coriander.

# Smoked haddock parcels
## with summer vegetables

*Serves 4*
*Ready in* 20 minutes

30 ml/2 tbsp olive oil

4 skinned smoked haddock pieces, about 175 g/6 oz each

550 g/1¼ lb/large can of new potatoes, drained and halved

100 g/4 oz asparagus tips

16 cherry tomatoes, halved

15 ml/1 tbsp snipped fresh or frozen chives

Salt and freshly ground black pepper

**1** Preheat the oven to 200°C/400°F/gas 6/fan oven 180°C. Cut out four pieces of baking parchment each measuring about 30 × 60 cm/12 × 24 in. Brush them lightly with the oil, then fold each one in half to make a square 'book'. Open out each book and place a piece of haddock in the centre of the square.

**2** Toss the potatoes, asparagus tips, tomatoes and chives with the remaining oil and salt and pepper to taste.

**3** Divide the vegetable mixture between the parcels, spooning it on top of the pieces of fish. Fold over the baking parchment, then twist the edges together to seal the parcels tightly. If necessary, secure with paper clips.

**4** Place the parcels on a baking tray and cook in the oven for 15 minutes. Remove the paper clips, if used. Tear the parcels open at the table to serve.

## Tips

★ Instead of the olive oil and chives, use 30 ml/2 tbsp of bought green pesto. Once opened, a jar will keep for about 6 weeks in the fridge.

★ You could serve this dish with some bought or home-made garlic bread baked in the oven at the same time. If you want to make your own, mix 75 g/3 oz/⅓ cup of butter with 2 crushed garlic cloves or 10 ml/2 tsp of garlic purée (paste), salt and pepper. Using a sharp knife, make cuts along a French stick about 2.5 cm/1 in apart, slicing almost through to the base. Spread each slice with garlic butter on both sides. Wrap in foil and bake in the oven below the fish for 15 minutes.

# Warm salmon and bean salad with Parmesan croûtons

*Serves 4*
*Ready in* 20 minutes

100 g/4 oz ciabatta, cubed

30 ml/2 tbsp olive oil

30 ml/2 tbsp ready-grated Parmesan cheese

200 g/7 oz fine green beans, halved

4 salmon fillets, about 125 g/4½ oz each

12 cherry tomatoes, halved

4 Little Gem lettuces

60 ml/4 tbsp bought or home-made ranch-style dressing

1 Preheat the oven to 200°C/400°F/gas 6/fan oven 180°C. Toss the ciabatta cubes with half the oil, then sprinkle with the Parmesan. Spread out on a baking (cookie) sheet and bake for 7–8 minutes until golden.

2 Meanwhile, cook the beans in boiling lightly salted water for 3–4 minutes or until just tender. Tip into a colander and drain thoroughly. Cover the colander with the pan lid to keep the beans warm.

3 Heat the remaining oil in a non-stick frying pan, add the salmon and cook over a high heat for 3–4 minutes on each side until just cooked. Set aside on a plate and break into large flakes. Add the tomatoes to the pan and cook for 1 minute, then turn off the heat and leave in the pan.

4 Separate the lettuces into leaves and divide between four serving plates or bowls. Top with the warm salmon, the beans, tomatoes and croûtons. Drizzle the dressing over and serve straight away before the lettuce leaves begin to wilt.

## Tip

★ For a simple ranch-style dressing, mix together 45 ml/3 tbsp of plain yoghurt, 45 ml/3 tbsp of mayonnaise, 5 ml/1 tsp of fresh or bottled lemon juice and 1 crushed garlic clove or 5 ml/1 tsp of garlic purée (paste) and salt and pepper to taste. Add some chopped fresh or frozen herbs too, if liked.

# Simple citrus salmon
## with spring vegetables

*Serves 4*
*Ready in* 20 minutes

450 g/1 lb baby new potatoes
Salt and freshly ground black pepper
200 g/7 oz fresh asparagus
200 g/7 oz fine green beans
15 ml/1 tbsp olive oil
Finely grated zest and juice of 1 lemon
Finely grated zest and juice of 1 lime
4 salmon fillets, about 150 g/5 oz each
15 g/½ oz/1 tbsp butter
15 ml/1 tbsp fresh or frozen chopped parsley
Slices of lemon and lime to garnish (optional)

1   Put the potatoes in a saucepan and add enough boiling water to cover. Add a pinch of salt and bring to the boil. Simmer for 12–15 minutes until tender. When the potatoes have been cooking for 5 minutes, place the asparagus and beans in a steamer over the pan.

2   Meanwhile, heat the oil in a large heavy-based non-stick frying pan with the lemon and lime zest and juice. When hot, add the salmon fillets, skin-side down, and cook for 3 minutes. Turn over and cook for a further 2–3 minutes until the fish flakes easily when tested with a fork.

3   Drain the potatoes and return to the pan with the butter, parsley and some freshly ground black pepper. Toss the potatoes in the butter as it melts.

4   Remove the salmon from the pan and place on four warmed serving plates. Spoon the juices from the pan over, then garnish with lemon and lime slices, if liked. Serve with the potatoes, asparagus and beans.

# Lemon peppered mackerel
## with sweet potato mash and curly kale

*Serves 4*
*Ready in* 20 minutes

4 fresh mackerel, filleted

Finely grated zest and juice of 1 lemon

450 g/1 lb sweet potatoes, peeled

225 g/8 oz potatoes, peeled

Salt and freshly ground black pepper

400 g/14 oz curly kale

10 ml/2 tsp crushed mixed peppercorns

15 ml/1 tbsp chopped fresh thyme, or 5 ml/1 tsp dried thyme

30 ml/2 tbsp olive oil

2 garlic cloves, sliced

A pinch of dried chilli flakes

1    Cut three slashes through the skin of each mackerel fillet, then put in a non-metallic dish. Sprinkle with the lemon juice and leave for a few minutes.

2    Cut the sweet potatoes and potatoes into small chunks and put in a saucepan. Add a pinch of salt, then pour over enough boiling water to cover. Bring back to the boil, then reduce the heat to a simmer, cover the pan and cook for 15 minutes until tender.

3    Strip the curly kale leaves from the tough stalks and steam them over the potatoes for the last 10 minutes of cooking.

4    Meanwhile, preheat the grill (broiler) to high and line the grill pan with foil. Mix together the lemon zest, peppercorns and thyme on a plate. Pat the mackerel dry with kitchen paper (paper towels), then press each fillet into the lemon-pepper mixture to lightly coat. Place on the grill rack and cook for 2–3 minutes on each side until cooked through and the skin is crisp.

5    Drain the sweet potatoes and potatoes in a colander. Heat the oil in a saucepan with the garlic and chillies for a few seconds. Return the sweet potatoes and potatoes to the pan and mash into the flavoured oil.

6    Serve the sweet potato mash with the mackerel fillets arranged on top and the curly kale to accompany them.

# vegetables

# &

# vegetarian

You don't have to be a vegetarian to enjoy the occasional meat- or fish-free meal, as these delicious dishes show. Everyone will enjoy Pad Thai Noodles and Easy Vegetable Lasagne. The recipes also include some high-protein foods enjoyed by vegetarians and you'll find tasty dishes for both Quorn and tofu.

If you don't eat meat, there are lots of other protein sources. But do make sure that you get plenty of vitamins and minerals in your diet, including iron; as well as eggs, other non-meat sources of this vital mineral include dried fruits such as apricots. Eating or drinking vitamin-C rich foods such as a glass of orange juice with a meal will help the body to absorb iron. If you're a vegan, remember that pulses and beans are protein-packed, especially when teamed with grains.

Enjoy the vegetable and vegetarian dishes in this chapter. They are full of flavour and allow you to take full advantage of the wide choice of vegetables from many different countries available in shops and markets.

# Pad Thai noodles

*Serves 4*
*Ready in* 15 minutes

250 g/9 oz dried flat rice (cellophane) noodles
30 ml/2 tbsp sunflower oil
A 500 g/18 oz packet of stir-fry vegetables
2 garlic cloves, crushed, or 10 ml/2 tsp garlic purée (paste)
1 red chilli, halved, seeded and sliced, or 2.5 ml/½ tsp dried chilli flakes
45 ml/3 tbsp light soy sauce
Juice of 1 lime
15 ml/1 tbsp caster (superfine) sugar
4 eggs, lightly beaten
*For the garnish:*
8 spring onions (scallions), sliced
50 g/2 oz/½ cup salted peanuts, finely chopped
60 ml/4 tbsp chopped fresh or frozen coriander (cilantro)
Wedges of lime to garnish (optional)

**1** Put the rice noodles in a heatproof bowl and pour over enough boiling water to cover them. Cover the bowl with a pan lid and leave to stand for 3 minutes or until tender. Drain and rinse in cold water.

**2** Meanwhile, heat the oil in a wok or large non-stick frying pan. Add the stir-fry vegetables, garlic and half the chilli. Stir-fry for 3 minutes.

**3** Mix together the soy sauce, lime juice and sugar and add to the wok or pan, followed by the drained noodles. Toss together thoroughly and heat through for 1 minute.

**4** Push the noodles and vegetables to one side and pour in the eggs. Leave to set for 30 seconds, then mix into the noodles and vegetables.

**5** Mix together the garnish ingredients with the remaining chilli and toss half through the noodles and vegetables. Divide between four warmed bowls and scatter the rest of the garnish over. Serve with wedges of lime, if liked.

## Tip

★ Cellophane noodles are transparent flat noodles that usually only require soaking in boiling water to cook them. Check the packet instructions, though, as some brands need a slightly longer soaking time than others.

# Easy vegetable lasagne

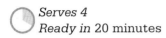 *Serves 4*
*Ready in* 20 minutes

20 ml/4 tsp olive oil

200 g/7 oz button mushrooms, sliced

400 g/14 oz/large can of ratatouille

4 sheets of fresh lasagne

15 g/½ oz/2 tbsp plain (all-purpose) flour

300 ml/½ pint/1¼ cups milk

15 g/½ oz/1 tbsp butter or sunflower margarine

Salt and freshly ground black pepper

A pinch of freshly grated nutmeg (optional)

100 g/4 oz/1 cup ready-grated Mozzarella or Cheddar cheese

Sprigs of fresh basil to garnish (optional)

**1** Heat 15 ml/1 tbsp of the oil in a non-stick frying pan. Add the mushrooms and cook over a moderately high heat for 5 minutes until golden-brown. Stir in the ratatouille and heat through until bubbling.

**2** Meanwhile, half-fill a heatproof bowl with boiling water. Add the remaining oil (this will stop the pasta from sticking together), then add the lasagne sheets, one at a time. Cover the bowl with a saucepan lid to prevent heat escaping and leave to stand for 5 minutes.

**3** Blend the flour with a little of the milk in a saucepan, then stir in the rest of the milk. Add the butter or margarine, then put the pan over a medium heat and bring to the boil, whisking all the time, until the sauce thickens and bubbles. Simmer for 1 minute, then season to taste with salt and pepper and the nutmeg, if using.

**4** Drain the lasagne in a colander. Place one sheet on a warmed plate, top with a quarter of the mushroom and ratatouille mixture, then drizzle with white sauce. Sprinkle with the cheese and garnish with sprigs of basil, if liked. Repeat for the other three servings.

*Serve with:* Garlic-flavoured or plain foccacia or ciabatta

## Tip

★ Fresh lasagne is a useful standby as it can be cooked by simply soaking in boiling water for a few minutes while preparing the other ingredients. It will keep in the fridge for about a week (always check the 'use by' date) or can be frozen, then defrosted in the fridge overnight.

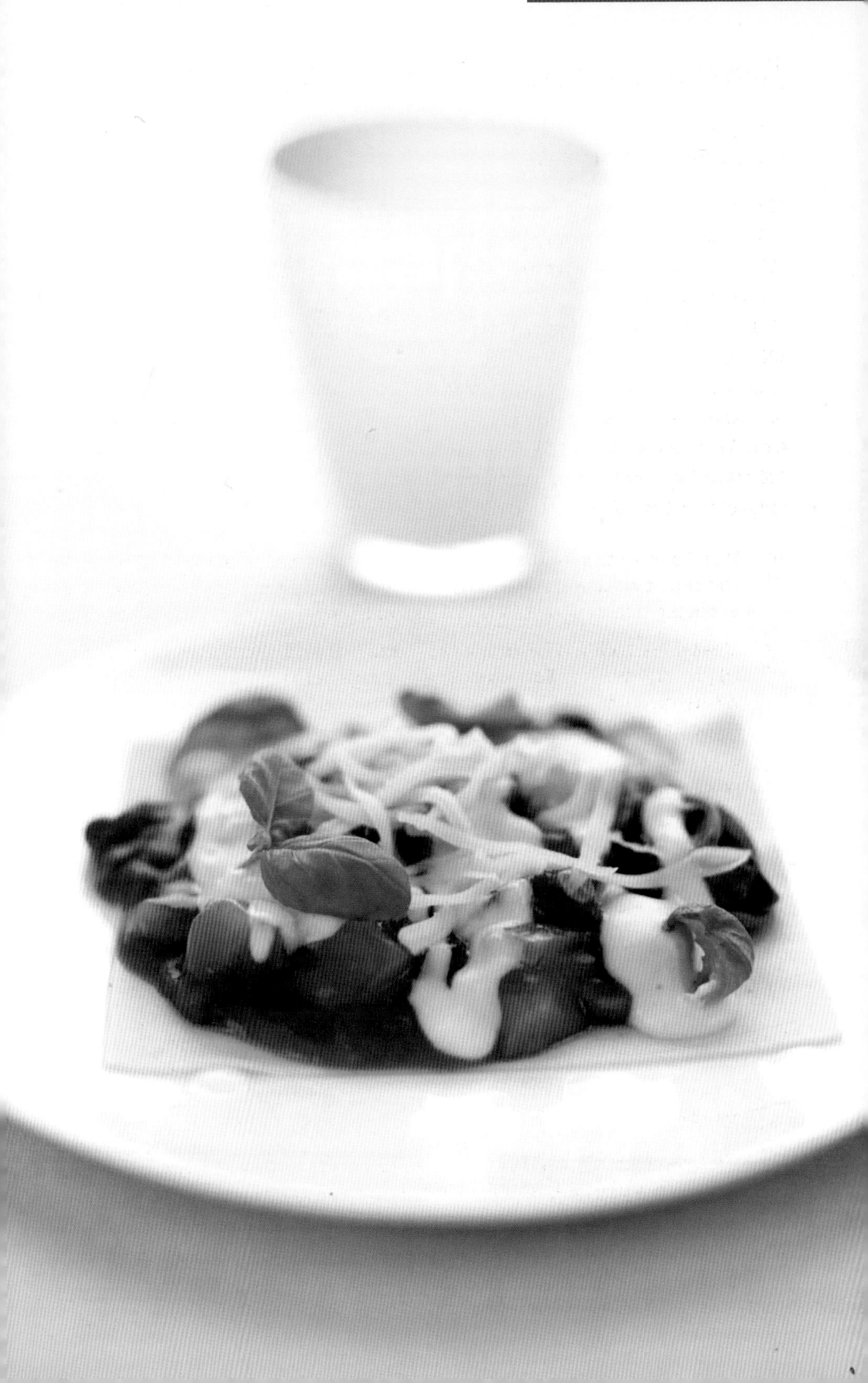

# Mediterranean vegetable pasta

*Serves 4*
*Ready in* 20 minutes

1 aubergine (eggplant), about 225 g/8 oz

1 large courgette (zucchini)

1 red (bell) pepper, quartered and seeded

60 ml/4 tbsp olive oil

Salt and freshly ground black pepper

A 500 g/18 oz packet of vegetarian stuffed pasta

75 ml/5 tbsp bought fresh roasted vegetable pasta sauce or tomato pasta sauce

**1** Preheat the grill (broiler) to high and line the grill pan with foil. Cut the aubergine into pieces about 5 mm/¼ in thick, 5 cm/2 in long and 2.5 cm/1 in wide. Halve the courgette lengthways and cut into 5 mm/¼ in slices. Cut the pepper quarters into 5 mm/¼ in thick slices.

**2** Put the vegetables in the grill pan, drizzle with the oil and sprinkle with salt and pepper. Using your hands, mix the vegetables so that they are all lightly coated with oil.

**3** Grill the vegetables for about 10 minutes, turning them as necessary, until lightly charred. Turn down the grill a little and cook for a further 5–6 minutes or until the vegetables are tender.

**4** While the vegetables are cooking, add the pasta to a pan of boiling lightly salted water and cook according to the packet instructions. Tip into a colander and drain thoroughly.

**5** Add the pasta sauce to the pan and gently heat until bubbling. Add the pasta and gently toss together, then add the grilled (broiled) vegetables and gently mix again. Spoon on to four warmed plates and serve.

*Serve with:* Crusty French or country-style bread

## Tips

★ As a quick alternative to the aubergine, red pepper and courgette, you could use two 250 g/9 oz tubs of Mediterranean-roasted chargrilled vegetables.

★ Use your favourite vegetarian stuffed pasta for this dish; pesto and goat's cheese or spinach and ricotta would both work well.

# Spicy vegetable pilau

**V**

*Serves 4*
*Ready in* 20 minutes

30 ml/2 tbsp ghee or sunflower oil
1 large onion, sliced
2 garlic cloves, crushed, or 10 ml/2 tsp garlic purée (paste)
15 ml/1 tbsp curry paste
½ cauliflower, divided into small florets
1 carrot, cut into matchsticks
1 red (bell) pepper, halved, seeded and sliced
350 g/12 oz/1½ cups white basmati rice, rinsed
600 ml/1 pint/2½ cups boiling vegetable stock
100 g/4 oz/⅔ cup peas, thawed if frozen
Salt and freshly ground black pepper

**1** Heat the ghee or oil in a large heavy-based saucepan. Add the onion and cook, stirring frequently, for 7–8 minutes or until softened. Remove half of the onion from the pan and set aside.

**2** Continue cooking the remaining onion for 2–3 minutes until golden-brown and slightly crispy. Remove and set aside for garnishing.

**3** Return the softened onion to the pan, add the garlic and curry paste and cook for 30 seconds. Stir in the cauliflower, carrot, sliced pepper and rice and cook for 1 minute, then add the stock and quickly bring to the boil.

**4** Lower the heat, stir in the peas and season with salt and pepper. Cover the pan with a lid and simmer for 10 minutes or until the rice is tender and the liquid has been absorbed.

**5** Leave covered for 2 minutes. Taste and adjust the seasoning if necessary, then serve on four warmed plates, garnished with the browned crispy onions.

*Serve with:* Popadoms and mango chutney

## Tips

★ Save time by using 450 g/1 lb of frozen mixed vegetables instead of the cauliflower, carrot, pepper and peas.

★ To add extra protein and texture to this dish, scatter with toasted cashew nuts or flaked (slivered) almonds.

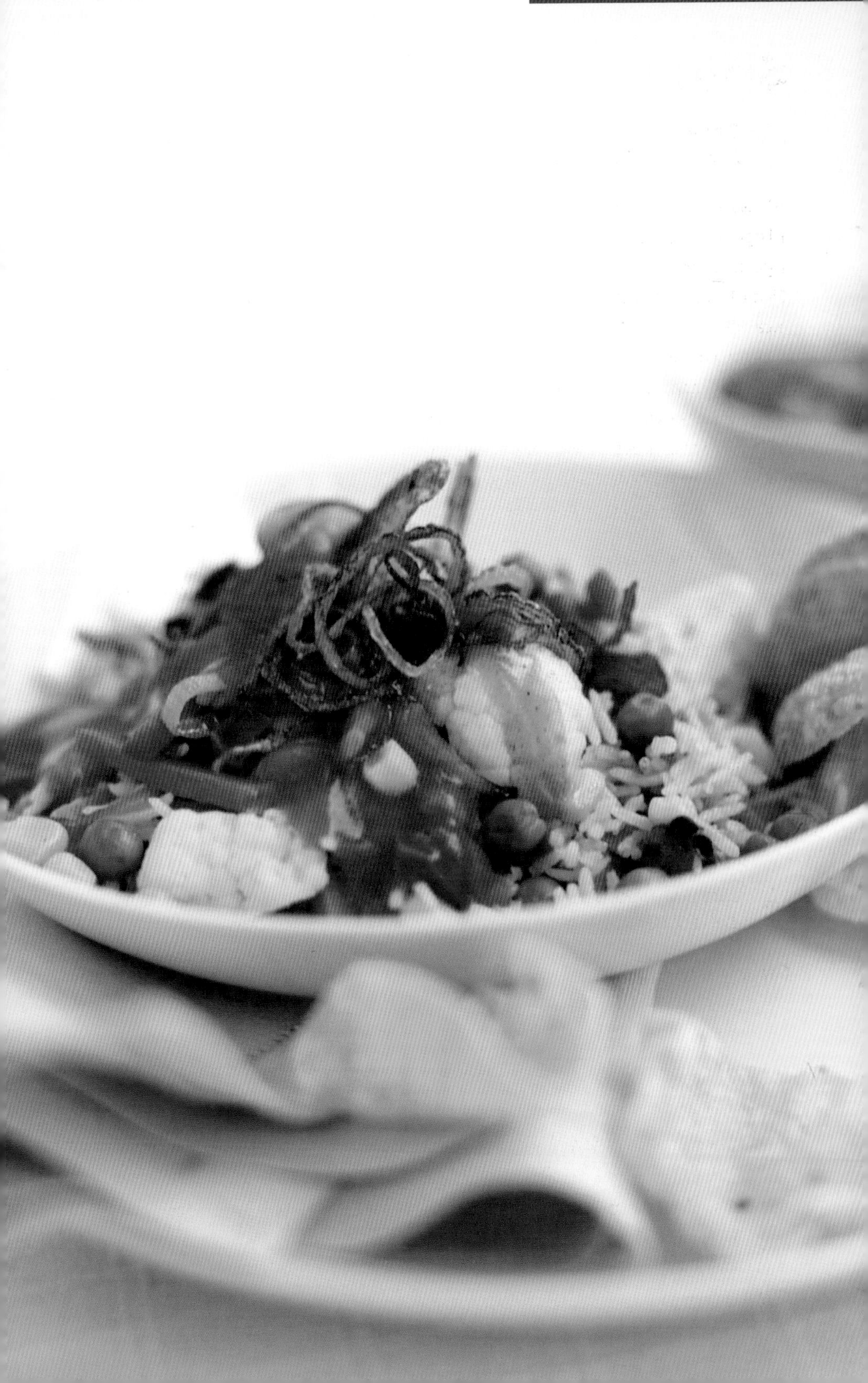

# Quick Quorn burgers

*Serves 4*
*Ready in* 20 minutes

45 ml/3 tbsp olive oil

1 onion, finely chopped

2 garlic cloves, crushed, or 10 ml/2 tsp garlic purée (paste)

45 ml/3 tbsp red pesto

A 350 g/12 oz packet of minced (ground) Quorn

75 g/3 oz/1½ cups fresh breadcrumbs

1 egg, lightly beaten

60 ml/4 tbsp chopped fresh or frozen parsley

Salt and freshly ground black pepper

4 burger baps

Shredded lettuce leaves

2 tomatoes, sliced

½ cucumber, finely sliced

Fresh coriander (cilantro) leaves and tomato relish or ketchup (catsup) to garnish

**1** Heat 15 ml/1 tbsp of the oil in a large non-stick frying pan, add the onion and cook over a moderately high heat for 5 minutes or until softened and just starting to colour. Stir in the garlic and cook for a minute. Tip the onion mixture into a bowl.

**2** Stir the red pesto into the bowl, then add the Quorn, breadcrumbs, egg and parsley. Season well, then mix everything together thoroughly. Shape the mixture into four burgers, each about 10 cm/4 in in diameter.

**3** Wipe the frying pan clean with kitchen paper (paper towels), then heat the remaining oil. Add the burgers and cook for about 3 minutes on each side until browned and heated through.

**4** Split the burger baps in half and, if liked, toast lightly while the burgers are cooking. Arrange a few shredded lettuce leaves on the bottom half of each bap, place the burgers on top, then the cucumber and tomato slices. Garnish with coriander and top with tomato relish or ketchup.

*Serve with:* Bought coleslaw or oven chips

# Mixed vegetable stir-fry
## with teriyaki tofu  **V**

*Serves 4*
*Ready in 20 minutes*

1 garlic clove, crushed, or 5 ml/1 tsp garlic purée (paste)
10 ml/2 tsp fresh or bottled grated root ginger
30 ml/2 tbsp dark soy sauce
15 ml/1 tbsp mirin or dry sherry
15 ml/1 tbsp clear honey
30 ml/2 tbsp sunflower oil
5 ml/1 tsp Chinese five-spice powder
1 packet of tofu, about 275 g/10 oz
250 g/9 oz medium egg noodles
A 300 g/11 oz packet of stir-fry vegetables
Fresh coriander (cilantro) leaves to garnish (optional)

**1** Put the garlic, ginger, soy sauce, mirin or sherry, honey, half the oil and the five-spice powder in a bowl and whisk together with a fork. Cut the tofu into 2 cm/¾ in cubes, add to the mixture and stir to coat. Leave to marinate for a few minutes.

**2** Put the noodles in a pan and pour plenty of boiling water over. Bring back to the boil, then half-cover the pan with a lid and simmer for 2 minutes. Turn off the heat and leave the noodles for a further 3–4 minutes to cook in the residual heat.

**3** Meanwhile, heat the remaining oil in large non-stick wok or frying pan. When hot, add the vegetables and stir-fry for 2–3 minutes.

**4** Turn down the heat a little, add the tofu and the marinade mixture and cook for 3–4 minutes or until the vegetables are tender.

**5** Drain the noodles and divide them between four warmed serving plates. Spoon the stir-fry on top and garnish with coriander leaves, if liked.

## Tip

★ Also known as bean curd, tofu is made from pressed soya beans in a similar process to cheese-making. It has little taste of its own but readily absorbs flavours when marinated. Try smoked tofu with almonds and sesame seeds for a change in this flavoursome stir-fry.

# Roasted vegetable salad V
## with Feta cheese and polenta

*Serves 4*
*Ready in* 20 minutes

1 red (bell) pepper, seeded and roughly chopped

1 green pepper, seeded and roughly chopped

1 yellow pepper, seeded and roughly chopped

2 courgettes (zucchini), roughly chopped

45 ml/3 tbsp olive oil

Salt and freshly ground black pepper

250 g/9 oz baby plum tomatoes

15 ml/1 tbsp balsamic condiment

300 g/11 oz instant polenta

60 ml/ 4 tbsp crème fraîche

50 g/2 oz rocket (arugula) leaves

150 g/5 oz Feta cheese, crumbled

**1** Preheat the oven to 220°C/425°F/gas 7/fan oven 200°C. Toss the peppers and courgettes in 15 ml/1 tbsp of the oil and a little salt and pepper. Spread out on a baking tray and roast in the oven for 10 minutes.

**2** Meanwhile, whisk together the remaining oil and the balsamic condiment to make a dressing.

**3** Remove the vegetables from the oven, add the tomatoes and sprinkle with 15 ml/1 tbsp of the dressing. Return the vegetables to the oven and cook for a further 5 minutes or until tender and beginning to colour.

**4** While the vegetables are roasting, cook the polenta according to the packet instructions until smooth and thick. Remove from the heat and stir in the crème fraîche. Season well and spoon into a serving bowl.

**5** Spoon the roasted vegetables over the polenta and top with the rocket and Feta cheese. Drizzle the remaining dressing over and serve straight away.

## Tip

★ Balsamic condiment is rich, dark and mellow. Originating in Modena in northern Italy, it is fermented from grape juice for a minimum of 4 years and the most expensive versions for up to 40 years. It has a unique flavour, so don't use ordinary vinegar as a substitute in this dish.

# Boston beans and vegetables

V

Serves 4
Ready in 20 minutes

15 ml/1 tbsp sunflower oil
1 onion, finely chopped
1 celery stick, finely chopped
1 red (bell) pepper, seeded and diced
1 green pepper, seeded and diced
5 ml/1 tsp chilli powder or 2.5 ml/½ tsp dried chilli flakes
400 g/14 oz/large can of baked beans
200 g/7 oz/small can of red kidney beans, drained and rinsed
200 g/7 oz/small can of chopped tomatoes
60 ml/4 tbsp cider or vegetable stock
5 ml/1 tsp dark brown sugar
5 ml/1 tsp dried mixed herbs
5 ml/1 tsp Dijon mustard
5 ml/1 tsp black treacle (molasses) (optional)
Salt and freshly ground black pepper

**1** Heat the oil in a large saucepan, add the onion and cook for 5 minutes over a medium heat, stirring frequently.

**2** Add the celery and diced peppers and cook for 2–3 minutes or until the vegetables are beginning to soften. Stir in the chilli powder or flakes and cook for 30 seconds.

**3** Add the baked beans, kidney beans, tomatoes, cider or stock, sugar, herbs, mustard and molasses, if using. Bring to the boil, then lower the heat, half-cover the pan with a lid and simmer for 5 minutes.

**4** Remove the lid and simmer for 2–3 minutes or until the sauce is very thick. Season to taste with salt and pepper before serving.

*Serve with:* Roasted potato wedges, microwaved jacket potatoes or Boston brown bread

## Tip

★ The black treacle isn't essential, but it is a traditional Boston bean ingredient and gives the sauce a subtle flavour and a rich dark colour.

# Quorn sauté with noodles V

*Serves* 4
*Ready in* 15 minutes

A 250 g/9 oz packet of fine or medium egg noodles

5 ml/1 tsp red wine vinegar

10 ml/2 tsp clear honey

10 ml/2 tsp dark soy sauce

15 ml/1 tbsp apple or orange juice

350 g/12 oz Quorn pieces

15 ml/1 tbsp sunflower oil

1 red chilli, seeded and finely chopped, or 2.5 ml/½ tsp dried chilli flakes

1 green (bell) pepper, seeded and sliced

100 g/4 oz mangetout (snow peas)

150 g/5 oz/2½ cups beansprouts

Slices of fresh chilli to garnish (optional)

**1** Put the noodles in a saucepan and pour plenty of boiling water over. Bring back to the boil, half-cover the pan with a lid and simmer for 2 minutes. Turn off the heat and leave the noodles to cook for a further 3–4 minutes.

**2** Mix together the vinegar, honey, soy sauce and apple or orange juice. Add the Quorn pieces and toss to coat. Leave to marinate for a few minutes while preparing the vegetables.

**3** Heat the oil in a large non-stick frying pan or wok. Lift the Quorn pieces out of the marinade with a slotted spoon and add to the pan. Fry over a high heat for 2 minutes until beginning to colour, then add the chilli, pepper slices, mangetout and beansprouts and cook for a further 3 minutes, stirring constantly.

**4** Drain the noodles and add to the pan with the marinade. Cook for 1–2 minutes or until everything is tender and heated through. Spoon into four warmed bowls and garnish with fresh chilli slices, if liked.

## Tips

★ Quorn is a high-protein, low-fat alternative to meat and can be found in the supermarket chilled cabinet. It is unsuitable for vegans as it contains egg albumen.

★ A 275 g/10 oz packet of plain or smoked tofu, cut into cubes, can be substituted for the Quorn, if you prefer.

# Index